Times Two

Two Women in Love and
the Happy Family They Made

Kristen Henderson and Sarah Kate Ellis

Free Press

New York London Toronto Sydney

fP

Free Press
A Division of Simon & Schuster, Inc.
1230 Avenue of the Americas
New York, NY 10020

The names and identifying details of some individuals
portrayed in this book have been changed.

First Free Press hardcover edition April 2011

FREE PRESS and colophon are trademarks of Simon & Schuster, Inc.

For information about special discounts for bulk purchases,
please contact Simon & Schuster Special Sales at 1-866-506-1949 or
business@simonandschuster.com.

The Simon & Schuster Speakers Bureau can bring authors to your live event. For
more information or to book an event contact the Simon & Schuster Speakers
Bureau at 1-866-248-3049 or visit our website at www.simonspeakers.com.

Manufactured in the United States of America

1 3 5 7 9 10 8 6 4 2

Library of Congress Cataloging-in-Publication Data
Henderson, Kristen.
Times two: two women in love and the happy
family they made / Kristen Henderson and Sarah Kate Ellis.
p. cm.
1. Henderson, Kristen. 2. Ellis, Sarah Kate. 3. Lesbian mothers—
Biography. 4. Lesbian couples—Biography. 5. Pregnancy. 6. Parenthood.
I. Ellis, Sarah Kate. II. Title.
HQ75.53.H46 2011
306.874'3092273—dc22
[B]   2010036477
ISBN 978-1-4391-7640-5
ISBN 978-1-4391-7642-9 (ebook)

Contents

To Thomas Tupper & Kate Spencer, our perfect storm

Remember what I said, as you lay down your head
The only thing we take with us is love . . .

—Antigone Rising's "Borrowed Time" (K. Henderson/N. Camps)

Prologue

From the beginning of our relationship, we knew we wanted children. Each of us had moved up the ladder with relative ease in our chosen career fields, so we naïvely thought the most difficult thing about getting pregnant would be making the decision to do it. We were wrong. First one of us tried, then the other, with no success. And then, all at once, we were *both* pregnant: on the same day, with the same donor, and with due dates that fell three days apart. Immediately, every single person we knew had one question: "How are the two of you going to do this?" Easy, we thought—there are two of us. One of us would run errands. The other would offer foot rubs. We'd rotate the late-night dog walks and order every meal in. Since we'd conquered the music business and the publishing industry, a little morning sickness would be a piece of cake, right? We pictured a sort of pregnancy fire brigade, each of us pitching in to help the other until we got too big, at which point we would . . . well, we hadn't thought that far. "Let's just celebrate!" we told our friends and family.

And thank God for our friends and family! It's like they knew when asking us the fateful question of how we were going to do this, the real answer was "You'll be helping us, sillies!" By the time we were in our ninth month, our home had a revolving door on it—with mothers delivering meals, siblings lugging baby shower loot, fathers assembling things they never knew existed, and friends dog-sitting and driving us to appointments.

Our grand delusions about the joys of pregnancy were squelched by the second trimester. Between the two of us, we experienced every pregnancy-related ailment listed on Babycenter.com, from numb hands to swollen ankles to inappropriately timed laughter. "I knew this was going to be fun," one of us would mumble sarcastically in bed, and the other would mutter, "I just had no idea how much fun," finishing the sentiment. Then we would roll over and snuggle with our individual body pillows.

But with our unlikely twins growing inside of us, every moment of those nine months taught us more about life—and our relationship—than any baby book, therapy session, or birth doula could. We learned, for example, that our mothers are always right. We learned that God has not come up with a better way to get a baby out than to have the body turn itself inside out like a tight-fitting pair of your favorite Jordache jeans from 1984. And that homeopathic remedies like moxibustion and traditional therapies like Pitocin and epidurals *all* work—depending on your definition of the word "work."

This book is our family's personal story. But in many ways, it's a story for anyone who has ever taken a pregnancy test and felt the heart-wrenching disappointment of a negative result. It's for families who would go to any lengths to conceive a child. It's for anyone who has ever been told their way of life is not acceptable. But mostly, it's for any woman who has fervently wished that her partner could just understand what it was like to be pregnant. Let this book be your empathetic partner, because our story redefines what it means to walk in another person's shoes. Trust us, we've been there . . . *Times Two.*

Times Two

Chapter 1

She's Leaving Home

Sarah

From the time I was young, I dreamed of being a successful businesswoman. In the seventh grade, I enlisted my friend Conrad to steal a copy of his older sister's science test. Knowing our teacher, Mrs. Truckenboat, never bothered to change the test from one year to the next, we then sold it to students for a buck apiece. In college I pursued more honest work: My best friend and I started our own business cleaning houses, walking dogs, and taking care of the elderly. Although we lost a dog and an old woman almost died on us, we still deemed the summer gig a huge financial success.

When I graduated from college, I met with a junior-level headhunter who helped me find an exciting job as an assistant to the associate publisher at the relaunch of *House and Garden* magazine. Working at Condé Nast was one big, heady party: I had a corporate credit card at my disposal and an impressive set of business cards. I was writing marketing proposals, managing events, putting gift bags together, scouting locations, and keeping schedules. Within no time I was promoted to coordinator; a year later I was promoted to merchandising and events manager. Eventually I needed more action, so I decided to work for a weekly and got a job at *New York* magazine. I was there just a year when I received a great offer to be the merchandising director at *InStyle*. Within two months of taking that job, I found myself lounging poolside in Lake Como, Italy, for our sales meeting. "This is how I like to roll!" I said to my coworker as we clinked our champagne glasses.

To the world, I looked like I was on track to achieving my dream—but inside, I felt like a fraud. I was gay and living two very separate lives. I worried that being "out" would hurt my career. Once in a while, if I knew someone was gay, I would say something like, "I'm going up to P-town this weekend," meaning I was planning to spend the weekend in the well-known gay enclave of Provincetown, Massachusetts. Later, that was the kind of coded statement that would annoy me when other women did it. But back then, *I* was the one dancing around the issue: I just wasn't ready to exist in the world as a gay woman.

I'm sure my hesitation to come out had something to do with my upbringing, which couldn't have been more traditional. I grew up on Staten Island, New York, in an area called Todt Hill, probably the most conservative neighborhood in all five boroughs, and one of the wealthiest. We lived in a Cape Cod–style house surrounded by a white picket fence. My older brother, Spencer, and I were sent to private schools and spent the summer swimming and playing tennis at our country club. If you need further convincing, my parents' names are Barbara and Ken!

Ken and Barbie Dream Houses and Dream Cars might have been popular then, but my parents behaved more like Carville and Matalin. They married right after college and were a classic case of "opposites attract." My mother was a Roman Catholic Democrat and my father was an Episcopalian Republican. They argued over politics constantly but had an immense amount of respect for each other; my father could get my mother laughing like no one else could. At the time, my father worked as a businessman in Manhattan and my mother was an elementary school teacher. Standing five foot eight, with a chic brown Vidal Sassoon bob, my mother cut an imposing figure in our household. She would never call in sick to work and believed in honesty and integrity. Babs, as we like to call her, had strong opinions on how to live your life. "Never rely on someone financially," my mother always told me. Every Sunday she took my brother and me to church, and as we walked past the pro-life activists collecting donations outside, she would say, "Don't look at them; we're not giving them money. Every woman has a right to choose—don't forget that."

Though I had a very privileged upbringing and was surrounded by love, I always felt like a piece of the puzzle was missing. My brother was always much more perceptive than I was; he would tease me and say that I was adopted, which I knew was untrue, but it would take years for me to realize why I felt so different. I had always felt most comfortable in the company of my girlfriends. Through my childhood and young adult years, I catapulted from one best friend to another: In fifth grade, Laura and I were inseparable, spending hours together creating volcanoes that erupted, riding our bikes around the neighborhood, and making each other "best friend" bracelets. In the seventh grade, enter Lisa, the swim team star: We traveled to meets together and kept time for one another when swimming a 1,600-meter race. That friendship ended in a spectacular scream-a-thon at a swim meet when I decided to hang out at the hotel with other team members rather than count her 1,600-meter swim. We never spoke again.

In high school, my closest girlfriend was Mia; she had the blondest hair and bluest eyes I'd ever seen. At five foot one she was petite, but she packed a lot of energy into that tiny frame; boys would trip over themselves trying to get to her. She was my best friend, so I had total access. I liked to talk about boys but had no real interest in dating any of them.

All teenagers are dramatic, but when these "fresbian"-style

relationships ended, I felt a crushing sense of loss. What I couldn't see then was that I was asking too much of these girls. They wanted to hang out at Baskin-Robbins and talk about boys. I wanted to hang out and talk to *them* . . . forever.

In 1989, I attended a small liberal arts college in upstate New York called Russell Sage College. My campus was only two blocks long, lined with brownstones from the late 1800s and enormous, old oak trees. My first few years of college were heavenly, full of fraternity parties, nights out with my roommates, and classes that challenged me. Yet something was missing. I would date men but it never amounted to anything. I found myself more excited to party with the reggae band at a fraternity house than to flirt with its members.

During my junior year, though, I did have a somewhat serious boyfriend. Chip, a conservative guy from Connecticut, fancied himself a wine and culinary connoisseur. If you didn't know how to properly let a bottle of red wine breathe, you might as well have spit on his mother. Our relationship ended in the summer when I finally realized we weren't a good match, and I returned to college ready to try something new.

The year was 1993, and it seemed as though the culture itself was conspiring to help me declare my identity. *Newsweek* had recently done a cover story called "Lesbians Coming Out Strong" that showcased a really attractive lesbian couple. The military's "don't ask, don't tell" policy was on the table. And Bill Clinton was our president. Suddenly a new thought crept into my consciousness: Maybe I should try to date a girl. But far from feeling that vast sense of relief that many people describe when their "light" goes off, I felt as awkward and confused as I'd been during adolescence. None of the stereotypes of being a lesbian appealed to me—a wardrobe of plaid shirts and motorcycle jackets, the love of granola and all things natural, not to mention a childless future. Still, I decided the only way to find out was to try it. So I decided to take a mature and measured approach: I targeted the "token" lesbian on campus.

I'd seen Becky around campus for years. You couldn't miss her: She had short, cropped hair and wore plaid shirts, pleated pants, and Doc Martens all year round. We were polar opposites—at the time, I favored floral tiered miniskirts and soft T-shirts—but what we did have in common was the only thing that mattered to me. I was determined to make her show me the way.

When I got back to college after summer break to complete my senior year, I was pleasantly surprised to find Becky sitting in the third row of my science class. I had no idea how to approach her, but as it turned out, I didn't have to give it too much thought, because my feet did the work for me. As soon as the professor finished going through the syllabus, I strode over to Becky's desk and gave her a big hug. Her face registered shock. I knew what I *wanted* to say: "Please help me figure out this gay thing!" But instead, I burbled frenetically about my summer and tried not to buckle to the floor with shame.

She must have sensed my nervousness, because she smiled and said, "It's great to see you. You're tan. Were you lifeguarding this summer?"

"Yes. I had, uh, a great summer," I stammered, blushing. "This class is going to be *hard,* huh?"

Becky smiled. "Could be."

"Science isn't my strong suit," I said, taking in her scuffed boots and the way she tipped her chair back while maintaining intense eye contact. "I think I'm going to need help to get me through this class."

"You want to be tutored, huh?" Becky said. Was that a smirk or a smile?

"Yeah," I said, adding, "We should probably get started immediately."

Over the next few weeks, Becky tutored me in her small off-campus apartment. She actually did have a knack for biology, but I spent most of our sessions focusing on how pretty her features were. We spent hours after our sessions talking about our upbringings, friends, and life in general. I tried to slip hints into the conversation, like "I'm straight but not narrow." When that had no effect, I was more direct.

Standing over Becky as she regarded my latest incomprehensible scribbling, I leaned in and said, "This girl thing is pretty hot."

Becky responded with a coy smile: "If you like that sort of thing." She was smart to play the game that way, because much as I wanted to do it, I was far too nervous to make a move.

One weekend in late October, a few of our mutual friends were taking a road trip to Boston. I knew Becky was going, so I enlisted my friend Marcy to make the trip with me. We arrived in Boston in the afternoon, and that night, we all headed out to a gay club called the Avalon. I proceeded to get very, very drunk—as drunk as any good lesbian would get on the night of her potential first kiss. I don't remember much of that night, except that I believe I danced on a banquette and somehow ended up with a stack of glow-in-the-dark necklaces around my neck.

It was three in the morning when Marcy, Becky, and I returned to our friend's apartment. Marcy stumbled off to bed while Becky and I shuffled into the living room to recap the night. I sat down next to her on the couch.

"That was fun tonight," she slurred.

"Well, if you think that was fun . . . ," I heard myself saying.

We sat next to each other in silence. By nature, I'm adventurous. I always want to try everything once. When I was younger, I liked to try dangerous things, like jumping off the roof of my house. This felt like a different kind of leap—one that led directly into my future. Feeling brave from the booze, I finally leaned in.

In that moment, I understood why all my straight friends had chased boys throughout my young life. That kiss was more than I had ever expected. I experienced a huge rush of endorphins and a feeling that it was "right." We made out for an hour and then went to our separate bedrooms, where I lay in a drunken, happy haze, replaying each kiss over and over in my mind.

When I woke up the next morning, I urgently told Marcy we had to leave. I didn't want to ruin the moment; I knew that with a whole day stretching ahead of me, I could only screw it up. First, though, I wanted to say good-bye to Becky. I found her standing over the stove scrambling eggs in the kitchen. I walked right over to her and put my hand on her arm and said, "That wasn't a mistake."

"Okay," she said. "Then we'll have to do it again."

Marcy and I packed up our stuff and hit the road. "What are you doing?" she kept asking me during the car ride home.

"I don't know, I don't know," I moaned.

"Do you think you're gay?" she asked.

I could only answer, "I don't know."

Marcy herself was a few months away from coming out, but at the time, she was just as conflicted as I was.

As with most lesbian relationships that form to help one person come out of the closet, my relationship with Becky should have lasted only a few months. We had so little in common. But she was my first, and I didn't know where to go from there, so the relationship lasted two years.

In 1995, I moved back to New York City. I was alight with excitement and anticipation, and yet I was still trying to figure out where I fit in. Where were the Yuppie lesbians—did they even exist? I certainly had not found them in Albany. At that time, I was twenty-three and just wanted to date. I had spent eight years of high school and college looking in the wrong direction. Now it was finally my time to try on different women for size. One night, I walked into a bar called Henrietta Hudson. And with that, I found the place I belonged.

Kristen

In many ways, I had a typical upper-middle-class upbringing: I grew up in a beach town on Long Island called Glen Cove. We lived in a big house with a pool that was a popular hangout for all the kids in the neighborhood. My mom taught English at my high school and my dad worked in advertising. But in other ways, we weren't so run-of-the-mill: My mother came from a huge Italian Catholic family—each of her parents had nine siblings, so she was literally one of fifty cousins. After my parents married in 1965, they settled down in the town my father grew up in. Surrounded by my dad's side of the family, my mom tried to give us the same childhood she'd had—filled with cousins, aunts, uncles, and Grandma Rosie's big homemade dinners.

My father's mother, Grandma Henderson, was the matriarch of our family and very much ahead of her time: She was vegetarian when nobody knew what that meant, taught yoga classes in her backyard, and held séances in her basement. She might have been the worst cook on earth—she'd leave a turkey in the oven all day only to realize she'd never turned it on—but was famously hospitable, hosting a huge, rollicking family dinner every Sunday night. Her two sons, my father, Frank, and my uncle Tip, took after Grandpa George—they were strong family men who were a bit more on the conservative side—but interestingly, out of the six kids they fathered, three were gay, and only Grandma Henderson seemed to have an inkling. When I was eight years old, I remember her pulling me aside and saying, "I love you, dear, no matter *who* you love." A strange thing to say to an eight-year-old, and yet her words allowed me to know, on the deepest level, that in this family, at least, I was loved.

When I turned four, my brother, Tommy, was born. I thought he was my baby. I would crawl into the crib with him, rock him, and dress him. Ever since Tommy came along, I knew I wanted kids:

I threw tantrums when I couldn't spend time with him and forced my parents to let me quit nursery school so I wouldn't have to miss a minute with him. As a teen, I signed up to be a camp counselor because I loved being around the kids. My ultimate goal was to work with children. But my *dream* was to be in a rock band.

For my twelfth birthday, my parents bought me a drum set. My older sister, Cathy, played guitar and the two of us spent every waking moment practicing together. Cathy got six other high school girls together, including a friend of hers named Jen who sang lead vocals, and we formed a band called No Comment. MTV was really hot then, and Jen and Cathy would pretend to be members of Duran Duran speaking with British accents to the press (that's how we came up with the name). We did great eighties covers like "Hit Me with Your Best Shot" by Pat Benatar. Our first gig was playing my aunt and uncle's wedding, but we soon became a popular little band around town. We played the Latin Club banquet at the high school, the middle school cast party for *The Wizard of Oz*, and a bunch of graduation parties. Still a seventh-grader myself, I spent my days rehearsing and hanging out with high schoolers, and I liked it that way. I was in awe of the older girls in the band, particularly Jen, whom I worshipped. With her long, thick red hair, she looked like a cross between Molly Ringwald and the pop singer Tiffany. I held her on a pedestal.

But my awe wasn't romantic; I liked guys. In high school, it never occurred to me to be romantically interested in women. In that regard, my ignorance was bliss, because a lot of my current lesbian friends really struggled in their youth. Of course, some of the signs were there: I was a tomboy who played soccer, softball, and basketball and was always picked first for teams. Fashion-wise, I hated dresses, and my uniform of choice was Levis, sneakers, and Champion sweatshirts.

My first boyfriend was a guy named Carlos. I met him through the older girls in my band just weeks before my sixteenth birthday.

My mom almost had a heart attack when she found out he was six years older than me, but I couldn't stay away from him. He was a huge track star who rode motorcycles, raced Jet Skis, and was known around town for skateboarding off curbs into traffic. He kissed me for the first time at my sixteenth birthday party, and after that, we were inseparable.

When I was a senior in high school, Cathy left to attend college at Bucknell University. My parents had met there, and it's also where my entire family—my grandfather, aunt, sister, myself, and eventually my brother—went to college. There, Cathy formed an all-girl band called Mistress for her Greek Week talent show. The lead singer was a girl from her sorority named Peppy, and when they couldn't find a talented enough drummer, I found myself traveling to Bucknell on weekends to play drums for them at parties. By the time I was accepted to the university, I was part of an established band on campus.

I dated Carlos all throughout high school, but we grew apart and broke up shortly after I arrived at Bucknell. My freshman year, I developed an instant crush on a senior named Hilary. Again, I didn't perceive my feelings as romantic, but I acted in ways that went beyond female friendship. I would go out of my way to position myself on the quad when I knew she'd be walking by. "Oh, what a coincidence!" I'd exclaim, fiddling with my Walkman. When she graduated and moved to Colorado, I went to visit her. And that's when I had my first crystal-clear lesbian thought. Oddly enough, it wasn't about Hilary, but one of her friends who came walking into the room and said hello. She had brown, wavy, perfect shampoo-commercial hair and her body was long and lean; she was a dancer. Immediately I thought, Oh my God, I want to kiss her. I was turning twenty and had never had a thought like that before. Hilary had to work the whole week I visited, so my days were spent four-wheel-driving, hiking, and picnicking with her friend. It never occurred to me to make a pass at her; of course, I wouldn't have even known what to do. Instead, I spent the whole week immersed in a mad, wild crush—one I figured would pass when I returned to school.

In 1990, Bucknell was a pretty conservative place. I was president of my extremely straight sorority, where all the girls wore choker-style pearl necklaces over black turtlenecks for their composite photos. Most of the students drove Saabs or BMWs, and we all wore Blucher moccasins from L.L. Bean, with our shirt collars turned up. But when I returned to school that fall, something in me had changed. I wasn't planning on becoming a lesbian; I just wanted to experiment. I thought I needed to kiss a girl and get it out of my system.

A girl on campus was rumored to be a lesbian; her name was Tracey. At the time, I was living off campus with Peppy in a four-bedroom house, and since Peppy was actually good friends with Tracey, I thought I'd float the idea.

One night we were hanging out in the living room and I said, "I think I want to have an experience. I want to make out with Tracey."

"Do it!" she said excitedly. "We can make a fun night out of it."

A week later, we invited a few friends over for dinner. I played guitar while Peppy sang, and Tracey stayed just a little too long. "It's late, why don't you crash here?" I suggested. "You can sleep on my floor." I had a futon chair that converted into a single bed. As I was pulling sheets over it I said, "You know, you don't really have to sleep on this. It's uncomfortable and I have a big bed."

Tracey gave me a sharp look. "You know what people have been saying about me. I don't want anyone to say I tried to turn the sorority president into a lesbian."

"I don't know what you're talking about," I said. "Just sleep up here. It's not a big deal."

"I don't know . . ."

Fifteen minutes later she crawled into my bed. It didn't take long to convince her to kiss me; she certainly wasn't resisting. I had my "experience" that night and it was amazing. In the morning, she left to go to class. I could hear Peppy and my other housemate Dabney moving around in the kitchen. My head was pounding but I remembered every detail. Half of me was filled with regret, while the other half couldn't wait to do it again. As I reflected on that first kiss, I felt overwhelmed. Holding my hand over my mouth, I ran into the bathroom and puked. Why had it felt like so much more than just an experience? Was I a lesbian now? I couldn't handle the thought, which seemed to nuke my ideas of marrying a Bucknell boy and having babies.

That afternoon, I called Tracey. "We need to talk," I said. "Can I stop by your dorm room?" As soon as I walked in the door, she grabbed my wrist and pulled me toward her. I resisted weakly. "Listen, this doesn't need to turn into anything," I told her. "I was just experimenting."

"That's okay," she said. "I'm cool with that." Boom—we were hooking up again. For the next year and a half, I spent my days flirting with guys and managing my duties as president of my sorority while sleeping with Tracey each night. There was no walking around campus holding her hand or "pinning" her with my sorority letters. I lived in constant terror of being found out. What scared me most was the fact that I knew I'd never been in love before. This was like nothing I'd ever felt.

Halfway through my senior year, Tracey broke up with me. "You pretend we're not a couple, so we're not," she said, her voice laced with disgust. "You're half-in, half-out. I can't take it anymore." I tried to protest, but she skillfully shot down every excuse I offered. I left her apartment destroyed; I knew I had no argument.

My roommates had no idea I was gay, but I could no longer keep my secret. My heart was broken, and I needed help. That afternoon, I spilled my guts to them. They tried to make me feel better, but I could tell they were surprised by my news. No one we knew was out. "I can't say I understand how you're feeling," my housemate Kara said as we talked over beers one night, "but I'll always be your friend, no matter what." Her words sank in like a tonic; she had no idea how relieved I felt after that conversation.

After that, I made it my mission to date another woman. And so began my Tarzan style of dating—swinging from one long-term monogamous relationship to the next. Before long, I was a very different person from the closeted, "I'm just experimenting" sorority girl my roommates had known from Bucknell. I wasn't alone in my awakening: It was an exciting time politically, too. Bill Clinton had promised to repeal the ban on gays in the military and a huge lesbian, gay, bisexual, and transgender (LGBT) march had just taken place in Washington, DC. I felt like I was part of a movement and wanted to submerge myself in gay culture.

Meanwhile, our college band, Mistress, was ready to re-form in New York City, with the addition of our friend Suzanne. But the name felt dated and degrading, so we decided we needed to come up with something else. Inspired by a Greek tragedy course Peppy and I had taken in college, we came up with the name Antigone Rising, after the Greek heroine who rose up to defy the king. We were all still working day jobs—my sister and I had jobs in advertising, just like our dad—but we ate, slept, and breathed music. The four of us lived within steps of one another in the West Village and played cover songs all night long in a little dive bar on Bleecker Street. We would start playing at eight P.M. and finish at three A.M., then go to work the next morning. Soon, we'd built a small but faithful following: We sold out bigger rooms like the Bitter End a few times a month playing original music. That led to gigs at Tramps, CBGB, and the Bottom Line. Within a year, we'd landed a manager, and we used our advertising connections to get magazine and media people to come to our shows.

In 1998, we got our first really big gig: a date at Lilith Fair. One of the sponsors of the tour, Levi's, held a talent contest at its Upper East Side store to find new bands in each market. We played in front of a panel of judges and won. Later that summer, Lilith Fair premiered in Bryant Park. I remember standing in an area between the stage and the crowd, with my best friend from college, Mitch, watching Sarah McLachlan perform. As I waited to go onstage, Mitch had me turn to face the crowd. "Do you see this?" he said, making a sweeping motion with his arm. "This is how it's going to be from now on." My dream was becoming reality.

That version of the band was together for ten years, including our years together at Bucknell. Then Peppy called a meeting and told us she'd given the band everything she could, but she wanted to move to Boston, get married, and have babies. I couldn't blame her. Even though we were selling out clubs up and down Bleecker Street, every major record label had passed on us. In July, we held auditions to find a new lead singer. We needed to find one soon, because we had a big gig booked in Chicago through BMI (Broadcast Music Incorporated). Our manager sent us the packet of a singer-songwriter who called herself Cassidy. "This is really weird; she said she used to sing with you guys," he said. Cathy and I opened up the envelope and pulled out a black-and-white headshot of an attractive woman with curly blond hair.

"That's the waitress from Houlihan's!" I exclaimed.

Six years earlier, when we'd first graduated from Bucknell, Peppy had taken time off from the band to complete her thesis. My girlfriend at the time was working at Houlihan's and told us the hostess, Cassidy, was a singer who reminded her of Peppy. For the next three months, Cassidy, Cathy, and I wrote and sang together. Then Cassidy informed us she was moving to L.A. That same day, Peppy called and said she was finished with her thesis and was headed to New York. Since then, we hadn't given Cassidy another thought.

Now we stared at the headshot in front of us. It was unmistakably the same woman. Cathy shrugged and said, "Maybe it's kismet." We popped her demo into the tape player and turned it on. Her voice, which we'd remembered as strong, had matured into a powerful, nuanced, knock-you-off-your-feet instrument. On some notes it was husky, others vulnerable—she sounded like a modern-day Dusty Springfield. Cathy turned to me, her eyes huge. "We've found her," she said.

I replied, "I don't even want to hear anyone else."

A few weeks later, the three of us met for coffee at a restaurant in the West Village. Cassidy seemed a lot more peaceful than I remembered. She had a Mother Earth vibe, with long, curly blond hair and an adorable smile. Though only five foot two, she seemed larger than life, as well as charming, funny, and comfortable in her skin. I could easily see her winning over our fans. For the next four hours we sat at a table in the window, talking about music and cracking each other up. We couldn't have envisioned a more perfect pairing. Not only were we like-minded, but each of us brought to the table exactly what the other person needed at the time. Cassidy's solo career was stalling, because she didn't have musicians to play with. I was still working a day job and frustrated not to be pursuing my dream full-time. I wanted to leap off the cliff but needed a little nudge. Cass was a bit of a rebel, unfazed about going without health benefits. "The money will come as long as you believe it will," she said, digging into her salad. When the words came from her, I was convinced.

By the end of the meeting, we were buzzing with electric focus. "From now on, we're going to do things differently," said Cassidy. "You're going to quit your day jobs, and we're going to jump in a van and tour."

"Screw the industry," Cathy added excitedly. "Who cares about shopping a demo and getting signed? We've created a huge market in New York; we can create buzz in other markets."

"We can do this on our own!" I said.

We were determined to.

Chapter 2

The Rising

Sarah

In the early nineties, you couldn't utter the words "lesbian" and "New York City" in the same sentence without mentioning Henrietta Hudson. A lesbian bar that stood on the corner of Hudson and Morton streets in the West Village, it welcomed a hip mix of women from all walks of life. At Henrietta's, I found women who were professional, young, smart, and attractive. I finally realized I could have bigger expectations for my future, as well as my future partner.

The first time I ever visited Henrietta's was on Valentine's Day in 1995. My college friend Darcy had recently moved to New York, and that night, we got dressed with a sense of anticipation. "I heard the girls there are hot," said Darcy as she spritzed herself with Calvin Klein's Obsession. I considered myself in the mirror: I was wearing a blue silk shirt and my favorite jeans; since it was snowing outside, I topped off my outfit with my mother's hand-me-down mink coat. Teetering out into the street in heels, we hailed a taxi, not knowing that the bar was a mere two blocks away from our apartment. To our disappointment, the bar was nearly empty when we arrived.

Before Darcy and I could even order drinks, a petite woman with long, blond hair walked up to us. "I'm Stacey," she drawled. "Can I wrap myself in your mink?"

Stacey was, at best, five feet tall, yet she made her presence known, firing off one hysterical one-liner after another. She introduced us to her friend Dina, a cute girl with dark, wavy hair and geometric glasses. After that, Henrietta's became part of our weekly routine: Dina and Stacey introduced us to their friends Lizzy, Christina, and Sophia, who all had cool jobs at MTV, top-ten law firms, and financial companies. We all had similar backgrounds: Our parents were still together; we'd attended private schools and enjoyed an upper-middle-class upbringing. The seven of us soon became inseparable, throwing extravagant birthday parties for each other, singing karaoke in Chinatown, having Sunday brunches, and planning trips to Cape Cod. Lizzy, a preppy girl from Wellesley, Massachusetts, with pin-straight brown hair and a ready smile, quickly became my best friend. She lived in a duplex apartment in the famed Archive building and worked at MTV. In her spare time, she traveled as the tour manager of a band called Antigone Rising. One night at Henrietta's, Lizzy introduced me to the band's guitarist: Kristen Henderson.

I wasn't very impressed. She seemed nice enough but not all that exciting. Still, when Lizzy invited me to one of her gigs, I decided to go. While in line to buy tickets at the show, I noticed a woman standing in front of me, talking loudly to her friend. "Ugh, what is this, the line to the bathroom?" she complained in a raspy voice. "This is taking forever!"

"Calm down, Sally," her friend said, glancing in my direction. I smiled and looked away. Then I stole a peek at Sally again. She was dressed in an Izod shirt with faded jeans; I noticed her yoga arms immediately. In fact, I noticed lots of things about her: The way she tossed her blunt bob back as she flashed a perfect row of teeth. Her minimal, expensive jewelry. Her groomed eyebrows, raised in a quizzical smirk. Too nervous to talk to her, I just smiled and went inside to see the show.

A few weeks later, Lizzy and I went to the Beacon Theater to see the Indigo Girls and who should I see in the audience but Sally. "I remember you," she said, pointing at me. "Apparently you have good taste in music." It was exciting to be singled out by Sally. She was dynamic, the kind of person who demanded attention without saying a word. We chatted between songs, and everything she told me further fueled my fantasies: She was a successful Hollywood producer with a Harvard pedigree. She'd traveled the world with celebrities and was just moving back to New York from Los Angeles after a breakup. She'd moved back east to be closer to her parents, so she could settle down and start a family. Sign me up, I thought; let's get this going. That night marked the beginning of a relationship that would last for the next five years.

At work, I was still deep in the closet. But I'd made a pact with myself that if I started dating someone I cared about, I would take her to meet my parents within the first month. Their opinion was the only one I cared about; I trusted them implicitly. But coming out to them had been no easy task. The year after I graduated college, I'd moved back into my parents' house on Staten Island. Each morning, my father and I would commute to the city together and talk.

One morning, when we were driving into the city, he turned to me and said, out of the blue, "Are you gay?"

His question was so direct I couldn't think of a way to deflect it. I looked him right in the eye and said, "Yes." I waited a beat and added, "Are you going to tell Mom?"

That broke the tension. "Well, I think I have to," he said, laughing. I will always adore my father for the way he reacted to my news. There wasn't a moment I feared I was in danger of losing his love. Many people admired my father; even though he had a huge job as CEO of a commercial real estate company he never used intimidation or scare tactics to get his way. I suppose that's part of the reason I felt comfortable enough to come out to him that morning in the car.

As soon as I came home from work, I knew he had already told my mom. She was sitting on the sun porch with her head in her hands, quietly sobbing. Seeing my mother that way broke my heart. She had always been so proud of me, and the last thing I wanted was to let her down. When she saw me she stood up and gave me an enormous hug. "I still love you," she said. "That will never change." I started to cry, too. I understood the source of my mother's pain: I was her only daughter. From the time I was little, she'd planned my wedding down to the last detail: Cocktails and hors d'oeuvres, but no sit-down dinner. A big tent in our backyard. A great band. In my mother's mind, that dream had just evaporated. Neither of us could know that life would grant her an even bigger dream.

After that conversation, no one talked about my sexual orientation again. We're Irish Catholics, after all. Six months passed. Then, at Christmastime, I broached the subject by asking if I could bring my girlfriend, Karen, to Christmas dinner. My mother looked flustered and said, "Why do you always have to bring this up?"

I had to laugh, because there had been no conversation about it since the day I came out. "Mom," I said as gently as I could manage, "I'll always bring it up." My mother smiled; she knew who she'd raised. She knew who *she* was, and I was my mother's daughter.

After that, little by little, the climate in my house started to change. My mother started to treat Karen like someone I was dating, not just a friend. My father probably got a little *too* comfortable: Sitting in his favorite chair, he would suddenly lower his newspaper and say, "What do you do if there's no penis?"

"*Dad!*" I would say, admonishing him. "Ugh, there are other things to do. Can we be done with this conversation? Please?" I watched my father shrug and raise his newspaper back up over his face. At least life was back to normal.

Kristen

In mid-August, Cassidy, Cathy, and I flew to Chicago for the BMI showcase, a huge conference celebrating women in media. It was a plum gig. We were each given our own suite in the Drake Hotel. "This is *awesome!*" Cathy exclaimed as she dropped her luggage on the plush beige carpet and ran around the room inspecting the floral couches, ornate lamps, and gigantic complimentary fruit basket.

That afternoon, an executive from BMI took us to lunch. "We're expecting about a thousand people," he said.

"Oprah is coming, right?" Cathy joked.

Our mood was happy and upbeat; the band was back on track. After lunch, we returned to our suites. Cathy's room was in a different part of the hotel, but Cassidy and I were across the hall from each other. "Want to hang in my suite?" she asked. For the next few hours, we laughed and talked, getting to know each other. I played her my favorite Shawn Colvin songs that I swore changed my life and she recited the Eddie Vedder lyrics she swore changed hers. Suddenly, Cassidy blurted, "I think I'm falling in love with you."

I felt my vision narrow so that all I could see was her face. "This is totally insane," I said. "But I feel it, too." Blame it on the wine, the five-thousand-thread-count sheets, or music itself, but what I felt was love. We ended up kissing for hours. As we prepared for our gig I warned her: "Cathy can't know about this."

"Oh, believe me, I know," she said. Neither of us wanted to put our brand-new band in jeopardy, but we couldn't control our feelings. To us, what had happened was inevitable and unstoppable, but we knew the rest of the band wouldn't feel the same way. I could envision Cathy's face turning purple as she screamed, "You're ruining things before we've even gotten started!"

That night, after our exciting show at the Women in Music and Radio event, I slept in Cassidy's room. We flew home the next day, giving each other looks across the aisle of the plane. For the next month, we remained in our cocoon of secrecy. But Cathy knew me too well. "Kristen," she said one day, "what's up? For the past month you've been totally checked out. I keep trying to call; you don't answer your phone. What's your deal? Have you met someone?"

I couldn't look her in the eye as I admitted yes, I had, indeed, met someone. "It's Cassidy," I admitted sheepishly, then waited for the ax to fall on my neck.

"Cassidy?" Cathy shouted. "*Our* Cassidy?" She just kept repeating those words, like if she said them enough times, they'd lose their meaning and wouldn't be true. "This isn't Fleetwood Mac, Kristen!" she added.

"I know it isn't . . . but it is now, a little," I said. "This will not screw the band up, I swear."

Weeks into our relationship, Cassidy and I moved in together. I quit my day job and cashed in my 401(k), and we found a place above a dry cleaner in New Jersey. We wrote some of the band's best songs as we inhaled the dry cleaning fumes in the little dump of an apartment. When I wasn't touring, I would write music and work on the band's website. The town needed a coat of paint, but Cassidy and I were in love, so every part of it seemed romantic. We would walk around the gravel track at the high school, cooking up schemes about what market we were going to conquer next. We would pick through bins at the local thrift store, trying to find outfits for the band.

In public, though, it was another story. Cassidy and I decided it was best to keep our relationship from the fans, from our managers, and even from our artist friends with whom we toured. Only our families, close personal friends, and bandmates knew. In fact, we had quite a large gay following—and tried hard not to alienate that base—but I was simply not ready to come out in a public forum. We also wanted mainstream credibility; none of us wanted to be limited by labels. Of course, our in-the-closet-with-a-wink approach happened to fly in the face of everything we stood for as a band.

During all the years we were touring, we were very accessible to our fans. Some would travel from city to city to see us—we knew their names, e-mail addresses, and favorite songs. Since we'd built a reputation as a tenacious, independent-spirited band finding a way to make it on the road, these "frontline fans," as we called them, would dip into their own modest savings to help us. They would throw gas money, Cracker Barrel gift certificates, and Starbucks cards onstage. At the end of a show, Cassidy would pull her sweaty bra out from under her shirt and we'd auction it off on eBay—within hours, the bidding would have reached $500.

Eventually, a management company that represented moe.— a hugely popular indie touring band—took us on. Their specialty was to help their bands build a following through grassroots touring efforts. They hooked us up with a big producer named Mike Barbiero, who'd done lots of work with Metallica and the Allman Brothers Band. In 2002, we started to record our demo. Meanwhile, our managers helped us to land bigger and bigger gigs. In Albany, where we were already somewhat known, we were invited to open for Joan Jett and the Blackhearts at a popular music festival. We played in front of twenty thousand people and had a blast. At the end of the show, my bandmates and I were still busy giving each other high fives when a woman approached us backstage. "I work for Joan Jett," she said. "She loved you. What do you say: Want to open for her again?" Obviously we were doing *something* right. Why rock the boat?

In April of 2003, Mike Barbiero called to tell us he'd brought our demo to a music executive named Jason Flom, who was going to come to our gig at Maxwell's, a club in Hoboken, New Jersey. Jason needed no introduction. As head of A&R (artists and repertoire) at Atlantic Records, he'd signed Kid Rock, Rob Thomas, and Twisted Sister, among many others. He made people famous, so much so that Atlantic Records eventually gave him his own imprint at the label: Lava Records. Though we were nervous before the gig, we played one of our best shows. We didn't even know if Jason had liked it, because he left without saying good-bye—or hello, for that matter. But the next morning, we got a call from one of our managers. "Jason absolutely loved it," he said. "He wants you in his office this morning." Within the hour, we were in Jason's office at Lava/ Atlantic Records to play for him and his entire staff. When we finished, they all clapped wildly.

"When's your next gig?" Jason asked.

"Tonight at Southpaw, in Brooklyn," I told him.

"Okay, see you there," he said. We left his office flustered and excited.

It became a tradition at our live shows for fans to rush the stage and throw money at us whenever we played certain songs. It was just another grassroots way for our fans to help us fill our gas tank as we traveled from town to town. That night, Jason was the one bum-rushing the stage and tossing us twenties. Later, he told us he loved the fact that we weren't going to bleed a record label dry, that we already knew how to book gigs and make it on our own. As soon as our set ended, Jason met us backstage, accompanied by a man in a suit. "I'm going to sign you, so you'll need a lawyer," Jason said. "Here's a pen. And here's a lawyer."

From that moment, we were no longer a small, struggling band—we'd been signed. All the hours of practice, the ramen noodle dinners, the relentless touring, it had all been worth it. Not that I'd ever had a choice. Signed, unsigned, Antigone Rising had always been my life. But for once, it seemed, I was going to be rewarded for my devotion to the band.

Sarah

From the very beginning of my relationship with Sally, there were signs that we weren't compatible. For one thing, she came from a WASP-y Main Line Philadelphia family. Walking into one of her parents' parties was like stepping into the pages of *The Great Gatsby*: The women were named Bibby and Mitsy and the men wore ascots and carried canes. Their way of dealing with Sally's lesbianism was to pretend it didn't exist. As her partner, I wondered, Where do I fit into this picture? Sally was also extremely driven. I would arrive at her house ready to hang out for the night, only to spend hours sitting next to her on the couch as she took a two-hour conference call. But I couldn't really blame her for the issues she had with her family or the fact that she had an important job. And she proved to be one of the most exciting people I'd ever met.

Soon after she returned to New York, she moved to Brooklyn with her two dogs. Though I loved my Gramercy studio, if I wanted to see her we had to go to her place because of the dogs. Holidays, too, became an issue between us. If I wanted to be with her for Thanksgiving or Christmas, it meant traveling to Philadelphia to celebrate with her family only. Sally often complained that my core group of girlfriends—the ones I'd met at Henrietta's—didn't like her, so I began to see them less and less in an effort to relieve the ever-present tension growing in our relationship. This resulted in conflict with me and my friends. "We know you're hanging out in Brooklyn now, but we never see you," Lizzy complained in an e-mail. When she confronted me for no longer coming around, I got so defensive I stopped speaking to her entirely. And Christina's attempt to have an honest heart-to-heart talk about how I'd changed since seeing Sally resulted in an irreparable fight. I knew girls weren't supposed to give up their friends for guys. Yet here I was, doing exactly that—albeit for a woman.

So, isolated from my friends, I tried to be happy in our little world. From the beginning, one of the things we'd talked about was having a baby. Now, two years into our relationship, Sally was ready to take the leap. Despite our problems, I was sure we'd be together forever. Perhaps creating a family would make the rest of our issues seem insignificant.

Around that time, I received a job offer, out of the blue. The events director at *InStyle* had taken a position at a new lifestyle magazine called *Real Simple* and recommended me for a senior director position. It would be a move up from my current post, with a lot of growth opportunity. *Real Simple* was only a year old, and I had loved it from its launch. As a new magazine, it was a risky move, but I took the job anyway.

A week before my start date, I got a call from my new boss, Grant. "A group of us are going out to dinner at Bubby's in Tribeca," he said. "Join us; it'll be a great opportunity for you to meet the team." When I walked into the room I was intimidated: Sitting around a long table in the middle of the room was a gorgeous group of young, fabulously dressed people. Francesca, the woman who'd recommended me for the job, motioned for me to sit next to her.

As I said hello and sat down at the table, everyone turned to me with a warm smile. Right away, I knew I was in the company of nice people. We ordered food and made small talk. Soon, the conversation turned to dating: Who was involved, who wasn't. Grant, who was gay, had just met a guy he really liked named Larry. "We just went on the greatest date," he was saying, but I couldn't pay attention—all the blood had rushed to my head. It seemed clear that I was going to be asked about my personal life next. What would I say? Sally and I were about to try to get pregnant. I knew if I didn't seize this moment to set the record straight, I was going to be playing the pronoun game for the rest of my career. And who would trust me in business if they found out I was a liar?

"What about you, Sarah—are you seeing anyone?" Francesca asked.

Before I could second-guess myself I blurted, "Yes, actually—I'm dating a woman named Sally. We've been together for a few years now." I sat there, my face burning, feeling as though I'd just signed my own death certificate, but to my surprise, the conversation moved right on to the next person. There were no dramatic pauses, no theatrical gasps; it was as though I'd said something normal. That marked the second big moment in my coming out to the world. But it wasn't cathartic or easy or a relief. I went home that night with my stomach in knots, sick that I'd revealed myself so openly.

A week later, I started my new job. Instantly, I knew I'd made the right decision. Our team was small, worked hard, and got along well. Grant became a mentor to me and taught me something new every day. I loved working alongside someone I could identify with personally and look up to professionally.

In the beginning of 2002, Sally had officially started trying to have a baby. Only my mother knew what we were trying to do, and she was attempting to keep a lid on her excitement. During that time, I moved into Sally's garden apartment in Brooklyn, which seemed to solidify our decision to be a family. I felt like I was moving forward in every area of my life.

One fall weekend, Sally and I drove to her parents' house in Philadelphia. That morning, we'd stopped by the fertility clinic so she could take a pregnancy blood test. We were in the car when Sally's cell phone rang. She answered, nodded her head, said, "Yes, uh-huh," and got off the phone. "It's positive," she said.

"Really?" I said, sucking in my breath. "Oh, my God—really? No, it can't be. You're kidding. *Really?*" I immediately called my mother. I had to hold the phone away from my ear as she screamed.

When we arrived at Sally's house, we barely made it over the threshold of the front door before Sally exclaimed, "I'm pregnant!" Her mother threw her arms around her, weeping.

Sally's parents were always kind to me, but they were conflicted about my role in their daughter's life. I received a very perfunctory "Congratulations" from them that day. At dinner that night when I said, "I'm going to adopt the baby," my announcement was met with awkward silence. Part of me understood where they were coming from; after all, coming out to my own family hadn't been the easiest thing in the world. But what I didn't realize at the time

was how much their opinions would shape Sally's world and, there-
fore, directly affect me. For me, having a baby was a pure expression
of love, not a political action. But when you're a gay woman con-
templating motherhood, you *will* be affected by politics—whether
you like it or not.

But none of that was apparent to me yet; I was just experiencing
the joys of joining a special club. Once the first trimester passed,
I told everyone at work that I was going to be a mother. I felt so
embraced and welcomed. Women stopped by my office to give me
their mom advice or recommend a stroller. In the seventh month of
Sally's pregnancy, my coworkers threw me a shower, and we oohed
and aahed over the bounty of thoughtful gifts: adorable outfits from
an exclusive Bergdorf's line, the entire bumper set we'd picked for
our baby's crib. The shower made me feel so accepted—so *normal*.

At home, things had vastly improved, since for once we were
focused on the same goal. Sally was exhausted so she eased up on her
work; we decided to move back to Manhattan and bought a duplex
in Chelsea with a huge backyard. On Saturday, July 12, 2003—Sally's
actual due date—her water broke and she went into labor. The following morning at 8:01 a.m., Gigi was born.

Sally and I spent the first night at home with Gigi in sheer delight.
Gigi was everything I'd dreamed of, but it didn't take long for brand-
new fissures to appear in my relationship with Sally. Within the
first few weeks, it became painfully apparent that our parenting
styles were completely different. Sally believed in feeding a baby on
demand; I felt a schedule was important. Sally wanted Gigi to sleep
in bed with us; I was terrified I would roll over and crush her. Sally
wouldn't let her cry anything out; I felt our baby needed to learn
how to self-soothe. When it came right down to it, there was little
we agreed on.

When Gigi was a few months old, I broached the subject of
adopting her again. Sally furrowed her brow and said, "Why do you
have to get all wrapped up in labels?"

"It's for Gigi's protection," I would say insistently. "In case any-thing ever happens to you. I know your parents will respect our arrangement . . . but what if they don't? I don't want to become a Lifetime movie."

"You always go *right* to the lawyer," Sally snapped as she changed Gigi's diaper. "You're being really paranoid."

And around and around the argument would go, until I was so confused I didn't know what I was fighting for.

Chapter 3

Love Walks In

Kristen

In the fall of 2003, we did a full cross-country tour, ending in Los Angeles. We stayed in L.A. for the next few months and recorded our first studio CD for Lava Records. By the spring of 2004, we sent fourteen final songs to Jason. He loved what he heard but was still in search of that elusive smash hit single, so he put us in touch with Rob Thomas, the lead singer of Matchbox 20. Cassidy and I wrote a song with him called "Don't Look Back," which eventually became our first single. Soon after that, we were invited to open for Aerosmith in a huge outdoor arena in New Jersey.

But the more successful we became as a band, the more Cassidy and I came undone. "It's your day off!" she would complain as she walked into the room and found me updating our website.

"We'll go out to dinner tonight, and I promise we'll discuss anything but the band," I said.

Sure enough, before the waiter could even pour water into our glasses, I'd already caught myself talking about the flow of our set list or how we could improve our mass e-mail system. *"Please!"* Cassidy would beg.

"I'm trying," I would respond. "I just can't shut my brain off." Suddenly, the same drive that had brought us together and given us so much success was now pulling us apart.

Our actual breakup wasn't a big blowup; it was more like letting the air out of a balloon. We were together on the road all the time, so we never got the kind of break that would signify the end of our relationship. But by August 2004, the writing was on the wall. Two of my best friends, Gretchen and Polly, invited me to spend a week at their house in East Hampton. When I left for the trip, I knew in my heart I was leaving the relationship for good.

That trip with Gretchen and Polly was the best thing I could have done for myself. We spent that week resting on the beach, going out to dinner, hitting the ice cream stand, and watching the Olympics on TV. "You changed a lot in that relationship," Polly finally admitted over dinner one night. "You became totally codependent. Honestly, I didn't recognize you." It had been such a long time since I'd heard a good friend speak the truth. We devoted the rest of the night to talking about what I wanted in a partner. It was obvious what I really needed was some serious time on my own.

When I returned, I stayed with my sister for a while and slowly moved my things out of our place in New Jersey. During one of those days, Cassidy and I ate lunch at a local diner. She admitted she was still attracted to men. I looked at her and said, "I'm finding that hard to believe." I don't know if my ego was wounded or if I was in a state of denial, but her words rang hollow to me.

She continued. "And I'm not in love with you anymore."

That was all I needed to hear. A week later, I moved into a house with Cathy in Glen Cove, the town where we grew up. My sister would have been well within her rights to say "I told you so." But she didn't. She just took my boxes off the U-Haul one by one and carried them inside.

Sarah

Being a first-time mother, I didn't know what to expect, but soon, I couldn't remember life before Gigi. Every one of her milestones was miraculous: smiling, crawling, pulling herself up, and eventually walking. I would spend hours rocking her in my arms, just staring at her and all of her little bits. Our connection was intense and immediate.

Yet underneath this wellspring of happiness was a gnawing kernel of fear: Sally and I were in trouble and I had no legal rights to our child.

On December 31, 2004, we held our second annual New Year's Eve party. Close to fifty of Sally's friends gathered in our back garden; I was still estranged from all of mine. We handed out fingerless gloves, built a fire in the fire pit, and played Ping-Pong until the sun came up. If Sally was distant that night, I didn't notice; I was busy running around refilling drinks and jumping into tournaments.

The next morning, I woke up with a headache and tiptoed to the kitchen so as not to wake Sally. Streamers and horns were strewn around on the counters; the sink was filled with dishes. I started to wash them when I heard Sally enter the room. "That is the *last* time I have more than two glasses of wine," I said. When she didn't respond, I turned around and said, "Hung over?"

Sally remained rooted to the spot where'd she'd entered. Looking at the floor, she said, "I need space. I'm not happy."

I put the dishes I was stacking down and said, "What kind of space?"

"I need you to move out," she said.

"Move out? What about Gigi?"

"Not forever," Sally said, looking out the window at the trees that greeted us each morning. "I just need some time to get my head together. You can still see Gigi as much as you want."

I walked out of the kitchen and into the living room and sank into a chair. "I can 'see' her? She's my daughter. I can't be away from her for one second. Please don't make me do this."

"Just for a few months," she said insistently.

I felt blood rise to my face. "Well, that doesn't work for me. I don't move in and out at your whim."

"I've done a lot of thinking about this and it's what I need to do," she said. After that, I couldn't listen to anything else; I could see that she'd already made up her mind.

In a last, desperate effort to change my fate, I said, "Please, Sally, please don't make me move out. If I move out, I'll never come back."

It wasn't until I said those words that I knew they were true. Up until then, I'd explained away—or just ignored—the myriad signs that we were over. I couldn't face the prospect of leaving Gigi.

I managed to stay in the apartment for five more months, all the while trying to convince Sally to change her mind. Then, just before Memorial Day, I took a sublet in the West Village. And that's where I spent my time healing. My parents drove in regularly from Staten Island to bring groceries, help me perform simple tasks, and talk me through the waves of emotion that had been washing over me every fifteen minutes. One moment I was filled with gratitude that Sally had the courage to end our relationship; the next I was in tears, feeling alone and miles away from Gigi, whom I was seeing three days a week. I spent my nights curled up in a chair, watching the moon move across the city. The relationship had been fractured for so long that I was constantly trying to figure out how to make it better. Now, with the admission that it was not going to work, I was free; I had a new lease on life. It was the best and worst I'd ever felt.

At work, I confided in two friends about the breakup and told no one else. Frankly, I was mortified. Everyone at *Real Simple* had been so supportive of my relationship, yet I couldn't make it work. To compensate, I became hyperfocused on my job, planning our next big marketing program. I didn't want anyone saying my work had fallen through the cracks, even if no one knew what was going on in my private life.

During that time, I got a phone call from Sophia, an old friend from my Henrietta days. We went out to eat and I told her that I missed all my friends. I didn't confess that Sally and I were in the middle of a breakup. I was so ashamed that I hadn't been able to make my relationship work and that I had also abandoned my girlfriends for five years. But Sophia didn't even mention it. It was as if she'd been waiting for me to return.

Kristen

By 2004, times had changed enormously for the music industry. Thanks to the advent of sites like iTunes and Napster, millions of consumers were downloading music for relatively little and sharing it for free. As a result, record labels found themselves fighting to control the revenue stream they'd once monopolized so effortlessly. But a little coffee chain called Starbucks had come up with a brilliant idea. The formula was simple: Place CDs at the front of the store and sell the customer music with his or her coffee. The idea was an instant success, and soon they were selling more records than any music label could. Their next big move was to partner with a record label and launch a debut album from a new band. In late 2004, Antigone Rising got a call from Jason Flom, who asked us to stop by his office to sing an acoustic set for the Starbucks executives.

We entered Jason's office to find a group of intimidating people in suits waiting for us—Jason, four of the top people at Starbucks, and Ahmet Ertegun, the founder of Atlantic Records. We were buzzing with nervous anticipation. We knew we were up against every new band from every major label in the country. Starbucks had commercial reach that far outpaced anything we could do to promote the band. This, we knew, could launch our careers.

When we started to play, everything unfolded perfectly. There were no mistakes. The songs sounded rich, melodic, and vibrant. We played the last note and held our breaths as we waited to hear the verdict. "Well," said one of the Starbucks executives, "I think we've found our band." We let out a collective whoop, hugging each other in disbelief. After years of touring relentlessly, scrimping and saving, this was it—we'd finally gotten our big break. On May 11, 2005, our live, unplugged acoustic album, *From the Ground Up*, was released jointly through Starbucks's Hear Music label and Lava Records.

How can I adequately describe what it was like to have a corporation like Starbucks backing our band? For two months, every single Starbucks franchise in the country had a huge Antigone Rising sign in the window and a kiosk full of CDs. You could walk into any store and find our music playing. By then, we'd built such a grassroots following that we had fans all over the country checking their local Starbucks to make sure our music was being sold. On the day the album dropped, we showed up in person to every Starbucks we possibly could, walked up to the barista behind the counter, pointed to the poster, and asked if it looked familiar. The clerk would spin away from the register and say, "Wait a minute, that's you!" Then someone standing in line would laugh, astonished, and pluck a copy of the album off the kiosk, saying, "I'm going to buy this right now." We enjoyed every minute of it and the label was thrilled. With the record out, our profile rose even higher. We were invited to play on the *Today* show and *The Tonight Show;* we became the Emeril house band on the Food Network for an episode; VH1 did a half hour special on us.

It was the most exciting period of my life. I'd gotten what I dreamed of, and the band was still intact despite the fact that Cassidy and I were no longer a couple. I just hoped we could all survive it.

Sarah

Through the grapevine, I heard that Lizzy was organizing a reunion for the Henrietta's gang the Friday before Gay Pride Day at a bar called Underbar, a swanky lounge in the basement of the W Hotel. I wasn't invited, but I knew my old friends were going to be there so I decided to crash it. Showing up, I knew, was making a statement. There had been chatter in the group that Sally and I had broken up, but no one dared to confirm it. By going to Underbar, I was telling the world the rumor they'd heard was true, publicly admitting that I'd failed. And that was my deepest shame, something that had kept me in the relationship long past its expiration date.

That day was gorgeous: blue skies, a breeze that slipped over your skin, a sun bright enough to demand sunglasses. As I walked through Union Square, I tried to calm myself. Were my friends going to welcome me or turn their backs? If they gave me the cold shoulder, I couldn't really blame them. I told myself that at least I looked good—there's nothing like the Heartbreak Diet. When I arrived at Underbar, I pushed aside the heavy velvet curtain that separated the hotel lobby from the entrance to the bar. I took a deep breath and made my way down the stairs.

Kristen

Since the release of the band's new CD, my schedule had been so hectic it had been nearly impossible to have a social life. Then my tour manager, Lizzy, called. "I'm throwing a party this Friday night for the old Henrietta's crew and you're coming," she said. I could think of no good reason to say no, so I drove into New York City to attend the event.

Festooned with red drapes and deep velvet couches, Underbar was the kind of place where you stole a first kiss or conducted an illicit affair. None of us could understand why we were sitting in a basement on such a beautiful day. As people trickled into the party, we decided we'd leave as soon as everyone arrived. Suddenly Lizzy pinched my arm, hard.

"Ow, that hurts!" I said.

"Sarah Ellis is here," she said in a loud whisper. Like Lizzy, I'd heard about Sarah's alleged breakup. I'd also heard about a fight Lizzy and Sarah had had a few years earlier; they hadn't spoken since. Lizzy hoped to make up with Sarah and wanted moral support. I turned and saw Sarah walking down the stairs.

Wearing a low-cut blouse, jeans, and slinky heels, she looked sophisticated and pulled together, like a young Jackie O. Why had I never noticed her before? I developed an instant crush. Sarah made her way through the crowd, hugging and kissing friends. When she got to me, I felt my heart do a little jump. "It's good to see you—I hear you're big-time now," she said, flashing a sunny smile. It felt good to see her, too. She'd known me since the days when I was playing shitty clubs, even if we weren't the best of friends back then.

When the group was complete, we spilled out into the streets and Sarah suggested we go back to her apartment. We walked together the entire way as she told me about Gigi, her job at *Real Simple*, and how she wanted more kids someday. I talked about the Starbucks album, my recent breakup, and my life on the road. On the corner of Eighteenth Street and Eighth Avenue, she paused to pull out a photo of Gigi. In it, I saw a little blond girl holding an ice cream cone in her chubby hands, chocolate dripping down her face. "She is *so* adorable," I said. Sarah beamed as she put the photo away.

That year, I'd created a list for myself that described my perfect partner: Someone very career-driven and independent, with a life of her own. Someone who wasn't an artist or a part of my band. Someone who wanted to have a family someday. Was it possible that Sarah Ellis, of all people, had it all?

Sarah

The chemistry I had with Kristen came as a total surprise. I certainly wasn't looking for a relationship—Sally and I had been broken up for mere minutes. It wasn't until the corner of Eighteenth and Eighth Avenue that what was happening between us registered. As Kristen looked at a photo of Gigi, she told me that she'd always wanted kids. Her smile was so kind and open, for a moment I thought, Could this really be happening? Is Kristen a possible partner?

Then I came back to reality. "But you're on the road," I said. She ignored my comment and we continued to my apartment, talking all the way.

Kristen

Ten of us squeezed into Sarah's kitchen. I tried to play it cool, but I was hopeless; every time I spotted her across the room I was drawn to her side. It's more accurate to say that I was following her around like a puppy, mesmerized by how she took charge of the group. I liked how she bossed everyone around. After we had a drink there, Lizzy suggested we move the party to Henrietta Hudson. "It's 'Reunion 2005'!" she shouted as we pushed open the doors and poured inside the familiar room.

Sarah

From the moment we reconnected that night, it seemed like Kristen was always at my side. I would walk over to the bar to order and there she was. I would stand by the pool table—suddenly, Kristen would appear. She actually scared me a few times. But she was making me laugh all night. At one A.M., I shared a taxi home with Kristen and Lizzy, who dropped me off on their way back to the W Hotel.

As I watched the cab pull away I thought, My God, I think I like that girl. It was a thought I quickly buried.

Kristen

It took a mere twenty-four hours for anxiety to set in. I wondered if what I'd heard was true, that things were over with Sally—but how over? A month? Two weeks? Two days? And then there was the issue of Gigi: There was a *baby* involved. This was no regular breakup. "Take it slow, Kristen," I told myself, knowing I'd never taken it slow in my life. I spent that night in a restless sleep, one moment flooded with fantasies of our relationship, wedding, future children, and then snapping back to reality.

The next time we met was on Sunday at the Gay Pride Parade. We all got together at Sarah's apartment. I was so nervous to see her; I felt like I was in junior high. Lizzy had told me that Sarah was interested, but I didn't know what her status was. We ended up spending the entire day standing on a street corner, trading stories about our lives. We were surrounded by jubilant crowds, yet it felt as if no one else existed. "I'm going on tour for the next two weeks," I told her. "More stuff for the album."

"That sounds fun," she said, smiling. It didn't seem to bother her at all.

While I was on tour, we stayed in daily contact via phone, text, and e-mail. "Mozzarella sticks at the Bus Stop Café?" I texted when I returned. That night, we ended up at her apartment, and for the first time, I tried to kiss her.

"I need to go slow," she said, moving slightly to the side. "My primary concern right now is Gigi, and I need to make sure she's okay." She bit her lip. "Is that okay?"

I immediately said, "Of course, totally okay. I respect you for it." And I did. She was a real grown-up, able to resist temptation in service to a greater good. In fact, the way she handled things totally turned me on.

I was ready to dive in, but for the next several months, the relationship progressed at a glacial pace. Rob Thomas invited the band on a six-week tour. Sarah and I exchanged hundreds of e-mails and texts and pulled all-nighters on the phone. During that time, the band had a week off and we were given some dates with the Allman Brothers. I had spent my entire life listening to them, emulating Dickey Betts and Duane Allman—and now my band was opening for them. I could hardly comprehend what was happening. One night during our run with the Allmans, Gregg Allman and Warren Haynes sat in with us. I could have died happy right then—but the best part was calling Sarah at the end of the night and sharing it with her.

By Thanksgiving, we'd met each other's families and had dozens of conversations about how much we liked each other. For me, those conversations were nice but unnecessary. As far as I was concerned, we were married.

Chapter 4

Like a Rolling Stone

Sarah

That summer, I was so happy that my feet never touched the ground. I had met the love of my life and was finally putting my long, heart-wrenching breakup behind me. At the time, my relationship with Kristen was mostly long-distance because she was constantly touring, but that worked for me; I needed the space and time. It was perfect: I now knew my dream partner existed.

By December, we were a solid couple. But my life was still in transition: I was moving from one furnished sublet to another, and each seemed progressively darker, drearier, and colder than the last. I was in a state of flux over my next move—an uptown loft or a downtown studio, a walk-up or a place with a doorman, whether to rent or to buy. Luckily, my parents offered to set me up in a room in their condo—they'd moved from the house I grew up in. Their stately and comfortable home was the ideal place to continue to heal. In the mornings, I would ride the ferry to work. In the evenings, my mother cooked my favorite dinners and insisted on doing my laundry. Whenever Kristen was in town, she would stay with us. Any discomfort my parents had had about the fact that I was gay was long gone. Moving in with them was the best thing I could have done for myself.

"So . . . what about babies?" Kristen said one morning when we were sitting outside on my parents' terrace overlooking the Manhattan skyline.

I glanced at her Allman Brothers T-shirt and said, "How could we do this if you're traveling all the time?"

"We can do anything we want; we'll get a tour bus for us and the baby," she responded.

"Sure, I'll just quit my job and tour with you guys," I said. "You have no idea what a big responsibility it is."

"Hey, wait a minute! Are you trying to talk me out of this? I thought you wanted kids, too."

"Of *course* I do. But we need to be realistic."

Back then, talk about babies was like pie in the sky, something we liked to dream about. I knew I wanted more children, but how we were going to get there, I had no idea.

Kristen

I spent the summer after I started dating Sarah traveling around the country, singing live at radio stations and doing interviews. I was still living on Long Island with Cathy—we'd turned our home into the band's headquarters and dubbed it "the Timber Shack"—but I spent every chance I got in the city with Sarah. I loved coming home to her dumpy sublet on Fourteenth Street, because I was coming home to *her*. At first, Sarah tried to keep me at arm's length—and I probably needed that, given my tendency to cannonball into relationships—but ultimately, she couldn't resist my charms.

Soon after Sarah moved in with her parents, I received an e-mail from our manager that said, "We're up for some dates with the Stones and it looks good." The Rolling Stones. For us, they were the Holy Grail.

I excitedly showed the e-mail to Cathy, but she, always the voice of reason, said, "The words 'looks good' are the kiss of death. You know how it goes: 'Hey, guys, guess what? You're going to be on tour with Stevie Nicks all summer! Oh, sorry—it's not happening.' So let's assume it's not."

A few weeks later, I was working in my little attic room under the eaves when I received another e-mail from my manager. The subject line read, in capital letters, "STONES DATES CONFIRMED." I read it once, then again. I got up, slammed my fist on the desk, and flew down the stairs without touching any of them. "We got it! We're touring with the Stones!" I screamed as I burst into the studio, where Cathy was strumming a guitar. We jumped up and down, hugging each other.

"Are you sure? Is this definitely happening?" Cathy asked again and again.

"It's happening!" I screamed.

Our first two dates with the Stones were in Chicago. The arena was gigantic—the biggest I'd ever seen. Often, when you open in a venue like that, no one is there, or the people who are there are restless: The crowd chants the name of the band they came to see and the lights are on. But that wasn't the case in Chicago. The house was packed, the lights were out, and the crowd was screaming at the end of every song. Ron Wood and Keith Richards were standing on the side of the stage, watching. During one of our songs, my sister and I came to the front of the stage to do dueling guitar solos. We looked at each other and started laughing in disbelief. We were playing guitar to twenty-five thousand screaming fans. Not too long ago, we'd been little kids, playing guitar solos on tennis rackets in our parents' dining room.

Our dates with the Stones were totally surreal. We were introduced to Mick in Baltimore, on the final night of our run. "Hey, ladies, heard you're fabulous; looking forward to seeing you tonight," he said. He posed for a picture with us and then he was gone. Later, while in our dressing room, Charlie Watts stopped by and warmed up with our drummer, Dena. I snuck a few shots of the encounter on my camera phone and e-mailed them to Sarah, who was sitting out in the arena with my cousin Kelly waiting for the show to start. Then the door opened and Sheryl Crow popped her head in to wish us luck. We shared the same management team, a fact that often made me pinch myself to make sure I wasn't dreaming. She'd traveled to the show with our managers, Scooter and Pam, who were all there to lend us support. I spoke to them in the mirror as I applied eyeliner: "Ron Wood invited us for a drink at the Rathskellar; it's one of the backstage bars they've got set up. Why don't you all join us?" Shrugging my shoulders, I quietly giggled in disbelief—not only at the words I'd just uttered, but at whom I was speaking them to. Sheryl and our manager Pam joined us for drinks, where we proceeded to tell Ron Wood that we planned to play his hit song "Stay with Me"—one he'd cowritten with Rod Stewart in the seventies—as part of our set that night.

"I'd be totally honored if you did that and I'll be watching you from sidestage," he said. Then he looked at me and said, "We have the same haircut, except you look much hotter than I do."

I high-fived him and gave him the name of my hairdresser, but it wasn't my last thrilling encounter with the Rolling Stones: As we came offstage that final night, I ran into Keith Richards, who was slinking around backstage. He had his sunglasses on and a cigarette dangling from his mouth. Looking right at me, he lowered his glasses onto his nose and said, "*Yummy.*" Normally, I'd flip a guy off if he said that to me on the street. But coming from *the* Keith Richards, undisputedly one of the greatest rock 'n' roll legends of all time, all I could do was blush like a schoolgirl.

Sarah

Life was starting to sort itself out in some ways: Sally and I had made it our mission to remain on good terms for Gigi's sake. Fortunately, it proved not to be a difficult task. We worked better as friends than we ever had as partners. Much to my relief, Kristen and Sally got along famously and were often the two making plans. A text message from Sally would pop up on Kristen's phone, "Meet us at Hollywood Diner," and within minutes we'd all be sitting around a breakfast table with Gigi ordering silver dollar pancakes and coloring on placemats. Afterward I'd take Gigi on my own for an afternoon at the Central Park Zoo or to her gymnastics class at Chelsea Piers, while Kristen and Sally would go off to the movies together.

As I was piecing together my new reality, my girlfriend was touring the country and living her dream. I loved that she had such passion, that she had an actual calling. But as we passed our first anniversary and with my thirty-fifth birthday looming in November, I felt a strong sense of urgency to move to the next level in my own professional life. One day, I was sitting at my desk at *Real Simple* when a friend of mine, Amanda, called and said, "Hey, Sarah, I'm in a rush, but I have just what you need." Amanda and I had spent long hours discussing our next career moves and she knew I was looking for a change.

I laughed. "Okay, I'm all ears."

"Remember that job I interviewed for, at *Vogue*?"

"The events position?"

"Well, I *thought* it was an events position, but it's not; they need someone to run the marketing department. I ended up telling them all about you, and they are really interested; you need to call them and at least have a meeting."

I thanked her for the lead and excitedly hung up the phone. I'd been working at *Real Simple* for five years. I *loved* my coworkers and my day-to-day duties, but this was a creative services director position, a huge promotion. And that position wasn't open at *Real Simple*—nor would it be any time in the near future. The fact that this opportunity was coming up at the exact moment that I finally felt ready to take a leap forward felt like a sign.

A few days later, I met with the associate publisher of *Vogue*. It felt strange to be back in the Condé Nast building, where I'd worked many years ago. There was a distinct difference in the culture and I noticed it immediately: more stiletto heels, coiffed hair, and looks up and down in the elevator. As I settled onto a cream-colored couch in the lobby, a pretty blond woman in a pencil skirt approached and introduced herself as Amber before extending her perfectly manicured hand. I followed her into the associate publisher's office. After greeting me with a warm smile, the associate publisher described the job: It involved leading *Vogue*'s marketing efforts and overseeing a team of twenty-five people. I felt that old, familiar feeling of excitement in my gut at the prospect of taking on a new challenge. Both my parents and Kristen agreed I should go for it. The next day, I gave my notice.

For the first time in my life, I was in charge of a huge team of people, making big decisions—and real money. I moved out of my parents' house and into a swanky rental apartment on Twentieth Street in Chelsea, with a view of the Empire State Building from every window. Kristen was touring, but when she returned in mid-October, she moved in.

"Kris, I think it's time to start trying for a baby," I said one day as we were sitting in our new favorite French bistro across from our apartment. "It seems like all the stars are aligning for us: new job, new apartment, new baby."

Kristen bolted upright and said, "I'm ready! I want *five* babies. Let's do this."

I laughed. "Let's start with one, honey. I think you should lead the search for the donor. It's pretty time-consuming, and now that you are off for a little while, you can check out the different donor sites."

"Perfect!" she cried, all but ready to flag down the waiter for the check and get started. I dug into my mussels and frites, making it clear that I was, at the very least, determined to finish my dinner.

I continued. "Here's what I'm thinking. We're both in our midthirties, so we don't have much time to waste. I'll get pregnant first, so you can release your CD and tour it for six months. Then, by the time I give birth, your tour will be over and *you* can start trying."

"I am so on board," she said. We kissed and clinked our glasses together, bouncing out of our seats with nervous excitement.

Kristen

Sarah and I discussed the idea of approaching a male friend or relative to be our donor but decided it might complicate our lives more than we preferred. Boundaries could be crossed; misunderstandings could take place. So in December, I sat down and started to Google our options. That year, we didn't have a new record out, so the band wasn't making much money. Financially, I was barely getting by. It was clear that I wasn't going to be able to finance the creation of our baby, but I was surely going to contribute sweat equity. I found the three biggest donor banks online and soon became an expert. I was astonished to find it took no more than the click of a mouse to hear these men speak and view their childhood pictures. I quickly became obsessed, reading through their essays and medical records. I learned early on that one donor could produce dozens of offspring, and this fact terrified both of us. So I conducted a relentless search hoping to find that rare candidate we could have all to ourselves.

Over dinner one night, we confided in one of our friends about our search. "Finally! You *can* have the perfect man," he said. The thought made us laugh. How could you possibly know this was actually your perfect man? Were they really submitting actual photos? Couldn't they lie about their SAT scores? And those schmaltzy essays! Who could possibly believe this twenty-two-year-old boy was donating to "help families who couldn't conceive on their own"?

There were certain personal traits Sarah and I were each looking for in our collective Mr. Right. Sarah wanted tall. I wanted smart. Sarah, who couldn't carry a tune, wanted artistic. I, having struggled and starved for years as a musician, wanted a doctor. We both wanted "exclusive," meaning our donor would give to only one family, and the only other kids he would have would be his own. That's where our journey to find the perfect donor hit a wall.

Exclusivity went against what these banks were trying to achieve. It was a business, after all. Their job was to find the best candidates who could supply the most product to as many people as wanted it. In fact, the banks, the doctors, and even most of our friends considered it imperative we use a donor with prior successful pregnancies. Sure, we understood that argument. We'd be spending a lot of money, so we needed to know that our "product" would work. Our concern was how we would explain to our future children that they could have several half siblings across the country. For some people, this was a nonissue, but for us, it was a dilemma that meant many sleepless nights. Of course, the banks did everything they could to offer us peace of mind. "Don't worry," they'd tell me. "We have regional quotas that prevent us from releasing too much of one donor to any particular part of the country." However, this method did not account for people moving from one place to another. As far as we were concerned, that quota needed to be one family per region, and that region needed to be the entire country. Clearly we would have to make a huge concession unless we could purchase a donor outright. And purchasing one outright could cost as much as a few hundred thousand dollars.

Our dream of finding an anonymous donor who was ours and ours alone seemed impossible. Until one day when I was going through the list of candidates for what seemed like the thousandth time and saw four exclusive donors listed on one bank site. I could not believe what I was seeing—I repeatedly checked the list. I had just been to that site a day earlier and no such donor had existed. I called the bank, and they told me that these particular candidates had dropped out of the program for various reasons. Due to their early departure, they'd left fewer deposits than a typical donor, which made them perfect candidates for one family to purchase. If one of the four fit your description of the perfect man, they said, you were in luck. And if exclusivity topped your wish list, you had better act fast; the bank made it clear that supplies wouldn't last. In addition to offering donor exclusivity, this particular bank also offered adult photos of their candidates. This was a huge selling point for us, as most banks only provided baby photos. Of course, the adult photo came with an additional charge, which we willingly paid.

Now, let's be honest. Everyone was a cute baby. The same cannot be said for adults. A receding hairline, a slightly crooked grin, the wrong shirt—any one of these things would break the sale for us. So we added the following question to the top of our criteria list: "Could we have dated him when we liked guys?" Two of the four exclusive donors were absolute nos. The third—who was of average height and looks—was a maybe.

But the fourth option was another matter. *Wow,* he has it all! I thought. It was a Friday afternoon. I couldn't wait for Sarah to get home from work so I could introduce her to Mr. Right. His boyhood photo was adorable. He was about six years old, posing for what I decided was his private school photo. He wore a navy blue blazer with oval elbow patches and had a hand in the pocket of his gray pleated pants. He was equally handsome in his grown-up photo, well-groomed in a collared sports shirt. He'd written a perfectly heartwarming essay where he spoke of his love for his parents and siblings, his superb upbringing, and his passion for sports and reading. He also stood over six feet tall and had scored a 1200 on his SATs. This was our guy.

As soon as Sarah walked through the front door, I told her of the miracle I'd shaken out of the computer: "*Mr. Right exists*—and he plays ice hockey!" It was something I never knew I'd wanted in a donor until I was able to have it. "He's everything we've ever dreamed of and he can be exclusively ours. The bank has sixteen vials waiting for us at *only* five hundred dollars a vial! Isn't that amazing?" Of course, I had yet to do the math: At five hundred dollars per vial, Mr. Right would cost eight thousand dollars to purchase outright. "You can't put a price tag on perfection!" I crowed, ready to hand over our credit card.

Sarah, on the other hand, seemed to be running numbers in her head as she stared at the screen. "He's interesting," she said. "I love that he would be exclusive to our family. Let's think about it over the weekend." She stood up and busied herself straightening up the living room. I was feeling impulsive. Sarah, clearly, was not. She needed the weekend to think about Mr. Elbow Patches. I would spend the next forty-eight hours selling him.

On Sunday evening, Sarah sat in front of the computer and began reviewing Mr. Elbow Patches' medical history. At twenty-two years of age, his medical sheet was mostly blank. He had not lived long enough to develop any illnesses. Other than his shortsightedness, corrected by lenses, and a little bout with acne as a teenager, we did not have much to go on. Even his parents' medical histories were brief. They were barely ten years older than us. And all four grandparents were still alive and healthy. Of course, these were all things I looked for in the donor, yet when about to make such a critical decision, Sarah felt leery. "How can there be nothing wrong with him or his entire family? Not even an aunt or an uncle has suffered from any major illness?"

"I know what to do," I said, and called my good friend Polly. She had gone through this process two years earlier and had given me some advice a few days ago that I wanted Sarah to hear.

"You will stare at the computer screen until you are blind," Polly said once she had the two of us on the phone. "You will read essays, debate about photos, and try to glean every speck of information you can from what little bit is given. None of it matters. A mental question mark will dangle over your computer no matter how perfect the essay or how handsome the picture. As soon as you start trying to get pregnant, you will forget all about Mr. Right. The process becomes about you making a baby for your family. And the minute you hold that baby in your arms, his two-page or twenty-page medical history will not matter. You will love your baby unconditionally."

We went to bed that night filled with excitement. We had found our donor and he had most of the traits we wanted. I planned to call the bank first thing Monday morning, so Sarah could start trying to get pregnant during her very next cycle.

As soon as the clock struck nine, I placed the call. I'd spoken to Marilyn at the donor bank several times, always with questions, but never ready to make a purchase. She was thrilled when I told her we had finally decided on a donor. I read her the ID number and she began clacking away on her computer. "Hmm," she said, sounding puzzled. "Can you hold on?" She returned a moment later to tell me the news. He was gone.

Gone? Just like that?

"Someone purchased him outright late in the day Friday," she said apologetically. "What about the other exclusive donors we are offering this week?"

"No," I said, wondering if she'd seen their pictures. "I'll take a look online and call you back."

I was crushed. It took me several days to shake off the loss. I kept checking back thinking maybe somehow he would magically return to the system. Sarah forced me to step away from the computer and stop obsessing. She tried to be sympathetic, saying, "Finding a donor is like shopping for a house. You can't fall in love with it or you'll lose perspective."

"Not exactly what I'm looking for in terms of advice, Sarah," I said. This process had turned her into her father. She was all business, pragmatic, with no room for hurt feelings. Instead of suffering in silence, I began sending Sarah photos of the least attractive and shortest donors the bank offered. "Okay, touché," she said when she called from work.

The following week offered renewed hope. I started searching other banks and broadened our criteria. Exclusivity was now off our list. We'd explain to our kids that someone gave our family a beautiful gift. And that it was possible he also gave a few other families the same amazing gift. With any luck, they didn't live too close by. And hopefully our best friends would choose a totally different gift from a completely different bank. We wouldn't say *all* of that, but at least the first part.

A few clicks into the new search and there he was. Blond. Gorgeous. He looked like Sarah's brother and he was a musician. We could hear an online audio interview of his voice.

Articulate, check.

Smart, check.

Funny, check.

I quickly developed a "donor crush." I couldn't believe how many traits he shared with both Sarah and me. Broadening our criteria had really helped. He blew away Mr. Elbow Patches. I called the bank and told them I had a few questions about Mr. Piano-Playing Handsome Blondie Man. And they answered. In fact, they started giving up more information than they probably should have. "He comes in weekly. He's so funny. All the girls at the bank adore him. He brings in coffees. He tells jokes. And he makes twins!"

"*Twins?*" I asked. "What do you mean when you say he makes twins?"

The voice on the other end responded, "Well, out of fourteen reported pregnancies, nine were twins. Isn't that fantastic?" Fantastic indeed, I thought to myself. Twenty-three offspring from fourteen pregnancies? Of which nine were sets of twins?

"Do you know where they're all located?" I inquired.

"Oh, they're everywhere," she told me.

"Everywhere?" I said. "Wow." I pictured smiling sets of identically dressed doubles stationed around the city. I sure wish I'd known that before I'd shelled out the fifty dollars to hear his perfect audio interview.

With that, exclusivity raced back to the top of my criteria list. I hurried to the site that offered exclusive donors and prayed all three would still be available. Quickly hitting the mute button on my computer as the site's annoying baby music began playing, I typed in the donor IDs. Sure enough, all three were still there. It seemed Sarah and I were not the only ones who did not like their adult photos. I stared at "the exclusives" from every angle possible, trying to find something, anything, that could make these men interesting to me. Then it happened. He wasn't drop-dead gorgeous or six feet tall. He didn't have the greatest IQ. His red hair *could* be considered cute. He admitted he was not the world's best athlete, but he liked playing sports. He had a brother he loved dearly, and he loved his parents, though sadly they divorced when he was young. And he was political; as a teenager, he worked on a gubernatorial campaign and loved the experience. In fact, the bank listed the governor's name. Clearly a mistake on their part, I figured, as they made it a point never to list identifying information. I researched the politician online. He was a Republican—and at the very top of his agenda was banning gay adoption. Exclusivity certainly comes with concessions, I thought. Exhausted from searching, I waited for Sarah to come home.

An hour later, she walked in the door and threw her bag on the couch. "Kris, you have no idea what's going down at work," she said. "It's crazy at *Vogue*. I had a sales rep crying in my office, telling me

her business is going to be ruined if I don't give her the right marketing program."

"About Mr. Piano-Playing Handsome Blondie Man . . . ," I said,
ignoring her rant. She stopped and gave me a frightened look.

"Don't tell me they sold out of him, too!" she cried.

"Oh, no," I laughed. "There is *plenty* of him to go around. Plenty.
He's made nine sets of twins!" I figured my sarcastic sales pitch
about the twin-making donor would strengthen Sarah's conviction
that our donor should be exclusive, and also soften the news that
our only exclusive option was a redheaded right-wing homophobe.

"Whoa, nine sets of twins? I'm willing to open our search, but
that's a bit wider than I'm comfortable with. Are there any exclusive
options worth revisiting?" Sarah asked with trepidation.

"I'm glad you asked that, honey." And so began my sales pitch for
the red-haired politician. "He's not that tall, but he's smart," I said.
"He was a cute baby, and his adult photo is all right enough." As I
pulled up his profile on the computer she still seemed interested,
but I didn't think she'd get past the fact that he'd worked on the
campaign of a governor who wanted to ban gay adoption. So I just
blurted it out. "There's one catch. He's a homophobe!"

"What do you mean, he's a homophobe? How could you possibly know that?" Sarah asked, looking closer at the screen to see if
this was listed as one of his attributes.

"Well, he worked on a political campaign for a Republican governor who wants to ban gay adoption, so he must be homophobic," I
said.

Sarah raised an eyebrow at me. "I don't know," she said. "I'm actually impressed that he's politically active. It shows character. I'd love
for our kids to feel passionate about politics when they grow up."

"But what about the part about supporting a *right-wing homophobe*?" I argued.

"I don't think it's so bad," Sarah said, unfazed. "I'm almost certain Republicanism is not a genetic trait. We both grew up in pas-

sionate political families who didn't necessarily share our ideals and I think it shaped who we are."

"And if our child calls him when he or she turns eighteen and is rejected?" I asked. "What about that?"

"You have a point," Sarah said. "We should call the bank and tell them our concerns."

The following morning I called Marilyn at the bank. "My partner and I really like this particular donor, but he worked on a campaign for a governor who does not support gay adoption. Is he aware that he may be donating to a homosexual couple?" I asked. "My children have the option to contact this man when they turn eighteen years of age. I cannot risk him having a negative reaction toward them. What do you think?" I did not want the process to drag on any longer, but I could not shake my worried feelings over this candidate's possible political views.

"I will call him and call you right back," Marilyn responded.

I was shocked. Call him and call me right back? You mean she was going to contact *him* and then contact *me*? Suddenly the distance, the anonymity, the degree of separation between us and our donor, shrank to one phone call. A few minutes later, my phone rang.

"He's absolutely thrilled to hear that a gay couple from New York City has chosen him," Marilyn said. "In fact, if you need him to donate any more for siblings, he'd be happy to come back to the clinic and leave samples."

"You *see*? I was right!" crowed Sarah when I called her at work to tell her the news.

Finally—we had found our man! He would arrive at our doctor's office in a few short days. At least, his samples would.

Chapter 5

Long Ride Home

Sarah

After finally settling on a donor, I started researching ways to get pregnant. I had stumbled across the at-home method: It involved lighting some candles, preparing a romantic dinner . . . then breaking in the middle of it to thaw five hundred dollars' worth of frozen specimen. After that, Kristen would blindly try to get me pregnant. Kristen loved the idea. I, on the other hand, did not. After all, this wasn't my first time at the rodeo. I knew what an insemination involved and there was nothing romantic about it. "Time is not on our side; we can't mess around here," I said. "We live in the middle of Manhattan, where we have access to the best doctors. We are having the procedure done at the doctor's office." At the sight of her disappointed face, I softened and said, "When it's your turn, we'll do it your way. You know I appreciate your 'open-minded anything can happen' take on life; it's one of the reasons I love you so much. Our appointment is tomorrow. Now go meditate on that, honey."

"Really funny, Sar. I can't meditate *for* you, though, Ms. Prag-matic. I'm sure you and the doctor will have an incredibly romantic thirty seconds," Kristen said mockingly, as she sunk into her best meditative pose and took a deep breath in.

The next day, we headed to the Upper East Side for an appointment at the best fertility clinic in the country. They took a sample of my blood, analyzed it, and gave me instructions to pee on a stick in two weeks, to detect ovulation. Then I was to return for my insemination. There was no guesswork or deciphering of instructions, just a skilled doctor using sterile equipment and extremely advanced technology to ensure I would get pregnant immediately. I figured I'd be pregnant in no time at all.

The first bit of good news came early on and was delivered by Dr. Mattingly, a handsome man who took his job very seriously. He seemed amused by my extensive line of questioning. "Preliminary blood work shows you're in great health," he said as Kristen and I beamed at each other. "Your FSH levels—that stands for follicle-stimulating hormone—are normal, which means your body is producing a good amount of reproductive hormones. I see no need to enhance your chances of conception with drugs or invasive procedures." I couldn't have been more pleased with his suggestion. Two weeks later, in February of 2007, I peed on my first stick to determine whether I was ovulating. When the purple line appeared, I headed back to Dr. Mattingly's for two inseminations on back-to-back mornings, to increase my chances of getting pregnant. I spent those mornings anxiously waiting in the lobby of the fertility clinic. On the first day, an hour and a half into my wait, I heard my name called, and with Kristen holding my hand, I was inseminated for the first time.

"Lie here for about ten minutes with your feet up, okay?" said Dr. Mattingly. He left the room and Kristen and I smiled at each other as I lay on the table.

"Can you believe you might be pregnant?" she asked.

"I know, it's so weird," I responded. After we checked out at the billing desk, we went to a diner around the corner to have breakfast.

"Are you having any cravings?" Kristen asked as I looked over the menu.

"Shut up," I laughed. "It's way too soon for that." Still, we couldn't stop ourselves from dreaming of the possibilities. We even debated a bit about whether we were going to have a boy or a girl.

That night, we continued the discussion over dinner at our favorite neighborhood restaurant. "Do you feel any different?" Kristen asked.

"No, not yet," I said. "Believe me, you'll be the *first* to know." Just in case, though, I didn't order my typical glass of wine. It suddenly occurred to me that we might be setting ourselves up for disappointment. "Let's not talk about it anymore; it's bad luck," I said abruptly. She agreed and we moved on to other pressing issues, like her band and my job.

Round one came and went with no pregnancy. Dr. Mattingly had told us that it typically took an average of three months to conceive, so we had no reason to worry over our first negative pregnancy result—or our second. By our third negative result, though, I was officially in a state of panic. Dr. Mattingly's office set up a consultation. "For your next cycle, I'm going to start you on Clomid," he said. I shot a pained look at Kristen. I knew what was coming. Clomid is an ovary stimulator used to increase the number of eggs produced in a cycle. I'd heard all about the potential side effects: severe mood swings, hot flashes, even paranoia. But with only a finite number of donor vials available to us, I needed to increase my chances of conceiving. Dr. Mattingly assured us that we had a great chance of a positive result.

Within two weeks, I started to experience my first side effects from the Clomid. One night, as I was walking through the front door after work, Kristen exclaimed, "Your eyes look crazy—like a rabid raccoon's!"

"I *feel* crazy," I said as I peered in the mirror. "Oh my God, I have red circles around my eyes!" Later that week, Kristen played a show at World Café Live in Philadelphia. At midnight, I looked at my watch: She was supposed to have called already. When the phone rang an hour later, I pounced on it.

"Where were you?" I shouted.

"I was—I was about to call you," she stammered.

"Sorry, it's probably the Clomid," I said, forced to admit it. But this excuse didn't put me at ease.

With each successive month, my symptoms only grew worse. I continued to hound Kristen about timelines: "I don't understand why I don't hear from you until an hour after your show ends if you say you're going to call me as soon as you get off the stage," I would say in an accusatory tone.

"If a show starts at nine P.M. we usually don't hit the stage until nine thirty; then after, we always meet with fans and friends," she would respond, sounding hurt. In the past I'd never given her schedule a second thought, but now I was trying to account for her every minute.

Kristen tried to ride out the wave of negativity by making herself as inconspicuous as possible, but since she had little to do at that time—she was waiting for her record label to give her the go-ahead to start recording—she spent hours playing video games in the living room with Lizzy. Whenever I entered the room, they would bolt upright and throw their joysticks to the side, like two teenagers with a bong who'd just been busted by their parents.

"I was just leaving," Lizzy would exclaim, stuffing her *Insider's Guide to Grand Theft Auto* into her knapsack.

"Totally missed you today!" Kristen would add with a nervous smile. One false move and I was ready to explode.

If I was making everyone uncomfortable around me, I certainly wasn't enjoying myself, either. The job at *Vogue*, while prestigious and lucrative, was hardly a perfect fit. In fact, it seemed to be the exact opposite. The huge team I was in charge of didn't seem open to having me there. I suspected there was something going on behind the scenes, politically, but I couldn't figure it out. There was a lot of infighting and posturing and positioning. At one point, it had gotten so bad the publisher hired a therapist to come to the office to give the senior management private sessions. All that drama seemed like nonsense to me. I had one thing on my mind: getting pregnant.

I'd been at *Vogue* for two months when I got a call from my former publisher at *Real Simple*. "Remember that marketing director position you wanted?" he said. "Well, it's open now. Why don't you consider coming back?" This was my dream come true: the place that I loved *and* the position I wanted.

It took another four months to work out the logistics, but by April I was back at *Real Simple,* albeit in a larger office and with a new title. I was thrilled to return to the job I loved, but at home I was still dealing with the horrors of Clomid. Generally, doctors recommend that women take the drug for only three cycles, but I was on it for six. By the end of that six-month period, I'd been reduced to an angry, paranoid wreck—exactly what I'd feared most would happen. Worst of all, it wasn't doing its job.

Fourth month: negative. Fifth month: negative. The fertility drug had drained me of my once outgoing and optimistic personality. At work, I started using a management style I didn't recognize, snapping at my team members for bringing me proposals a day later than they had promised. My relationship with Kristen had been reduced to nothing more than achieving one goal. We could think of nothing else. News of our friends' pregnancies left us feeling jealous and angry. We lived with a tension that had never been present before in our relationship. And we began to question whether we really should start a family.

In the sixth month, Dr. Mattingly gave us an ultimatum: Find a new donor or move to a much more aggressive form of fertility treatment, IVF, or in-vitro fertilization. This method involved controlling the ovulatory process with hormones, surgically removing the eggs and fertilizing them outside the body, then returning them to the uterus. It was the treatment to turn to when all other methods had failed. It wasn't only surgically invasive, it also required a potent form of drug therapy for two months leading up to the procedure. I didn't know if I could stand to try another drug, though I had to admit that nothing could be worse than Clomid.

From the beginning, Kristen had reluctantly agreed to the modern medical approach to making our baby. Since I had been ruled perfectly healthy and capable of conceiving, she found no good reason to trek up to a doctor's office several times a month when we could do it from the comfort of our own home. Plus, after too many months on fertility drugs, I was severely depressed. "I think we should rethink the at-home approach," Kristen said.

"Not yet." I sighed. "Not before finding a new donor." So Kristen fired up the computer again. After spending eight thousand dollars on Mr. Exclusive, we were now faced with the task of finding our true Mr. Right. The new search gave us renewed hope and helped settle our hidden anxieties. Kristen had secretly worried Mr. Exclusive's political affiliation was an inherited trait, and I had been genuinely concerned with his short stature.

We went directly to the bank's website and punched in our two favorite traits: six feet tall and high SAT scores. Four options popped up on the screen. Two of the candidates were ruled out instantly due to their lackluster adult photos. The two remaining options were both tall and handsome, but we favored one over the other. He had a dimple in his cheek and a backward baseball cap on his head; something about his photo felt familiar to us.

"He reminds me of your cousin," I said to Kristen.

"That's funny," she replied. "He reminds me of your brother!"

It turned out he was brand-new to the system and had no prior pregnancies. He was athletic and musical with brown hair and green eyes, and we were also impressed with his essay. He'd listed drawing and reading as hobbies. He came from a loving family, his parents were still married, there were no serious medical issues in his history, and he was willing to be contacted when the children turned eighteen. By the time we finished reading his page we had made our decision. His samples would be shipped out that night.

The following morning, Dr. Mattingly entered the exam room, snapped on a pair of rubber gloves, rolled up his chair and announced, "This guy's numbers are way better than the last one. We've got one hundred and eighty million . . ." His voice trailed off in my head as I stared up at the light above the exam table. Finally, I thought—this is it. Our baby was on the way. It seemed that fate, or God, or the universe had intervened to send the appropriate donor. Our former little Alex P. Keaton would remain a mere idea.

"That's it, Sarah, you're done," Dr. Mattingly said. "Just lie here for twenty minutes." He got up and left the room.

Month six: negative. Months seven and eight: negative and negative. Kristen had a theory for every negative stick: "This doctor's office is too stressful. It's too cold and impersonal. Maybe your body can't get pregnant this early in the morning. Time of day *has* to be a factor."

Our doctors tried to comfort me by saying, "It's not an exact science, Sarah. We see things like this from time to time."

But Kristen was convinced that stress was getting in the way: "They jack you up on mood-altering drugs for six months, watch us spend tens of thousands of dollars on donors, force us to sit in a waiting room for two hours twice a month, and you *wonder* why your body can't get pregnant?"

"They want me to do an IVF cycle next," I told her.

Kristen shook her head. "We're doing it from home," she said. "I'll figure it out."

Kristen

At that point, Sarah and I were all business. She seemed totally different from the woman I fell in love with. Trying my best not to

make the situation worse, I hid my disappointment about the negative results, but I was feeling very isolated. I could now understand
what some husbands felt when their wives tried to get pregnant:
eager to contribute but unable to do much more than helplessly
stand by. That's why I loved the idea of doing it from home. Finally, I
would have a real role in the process.

Ten years earlier, a music producer I'd worked with had inseminated her partner at home, producing a healthy baby girl. They were
the first lesbian couple I'd ever known to have a baby, so their experience became my benchmark. Several of Sarah's lesbian friends had
children, but none of them had conceived at home. So our experiences with various fertility methods had created opposing beliefs.
Skeptical of our doctor's insistence that we should embark on a procedure reserved for women diagnosed with serious fertility issues,
Sarah finally allowed me to explore the at-home option.

I called my music producer friend for advice and she briskly ran
through most of my questions until I got to the most important
one. "How do you thaw the vial?" I asked.

"You know what, I have no idea," she responded. "It was so long
ago, I can't remember. It couldn't have been that difficult, though,
because we have two daughters."

I laughed, reassured. And yet I still couldn't find one legitimate
website explaining how to transport the tissue specimen—much
less one that explained how to thaw it. "Okay, we're flying blind,"
I muttered to myself, then shut down the computer. Hadn't human
beings navigated life without the Internet for decades?

I called Marilyn at the donor bank and arranged to have our
specimen shipped directly to our house. "It can only be shipped to a
proper tissue-storing facility and only with notarized consent from
your doctor," she said. "You will need to transport it in a cryogenic
tank filled with nitrous oxide to keep the specimen frozen at the
proper temperature."

I was intimidated and overwhelmed by the obstacles involved

with an at-home shipment. On a deeper level, I was struggling with the idea of having to explain what we were doing to stranger after stranger. Sometimes it felt like I was wearing a neon sign around my neck that read, "I'm doing this at home because *I'm a big lesbian!*" There was some good news, though. Marilyn informed me that the lab would ship the specimen with thawing instructions. One problem solved. Now I had to find a tissue-storage facility willing to accept our delivery and allow me to pick it up. As a prideful resident of New York City, I believed anything could be accomplished within its borders, but this task felt daunting even for Gotham. Fortunately, I was wrong. There was a facility ten blocks north of my apartment. I gave them a call and immediately began stumbling over my words: "Hi, I have a few strange questions for you," I said. "I need to have our, mine and my partner's, our, uh, sperm specimen samples shipped."

"Shipped to us so you can pick it up? Just have your bank take care of it," the woman who answered the phone said, as though she had this conversation every day. (Well, I suppose she did.) She continued. "We will need a certified letter from your doctor granting you permission to take the tissue from our facility. We will provide you with a tank filled with nitrous oxide, which will keep your specimen frozen for seven full days. When you get here we will take you through the process of transporting and thawing. And we will give you instructions on how to handle it all from home. When should we expect you?"

"In two days," I replied, impressed with my own problem-solving skills. "I'll call my bank with your address."

"They should have our address. Just tell them the name of our facility."

"Great. Thanks," I said. She made the process sound so easy. Then I remembered a very important question: "Oh! One more thing. How much will this cost?"

"Five hundred dollars to rent the nitrous oxide tank for a week, two hundred and fifty dollars for us to handle and receive the ship-ment, and a two-hundred-and-fifty-dollar monthly storage fee for any vials you leave with us."

I ran through a dizzying array of numbers in my head, trying to figure out how long it would be before we were bankrupt. "Thank you," I responded. "See you in two days." What had felt like a monu-mental, unsolvable dilemma had been fully resolved in less than ten minutes.

Now came the final task to research: home insemination. I had heard of the "turkey baster method" crudely referred to in books and on TV, but I didn't think that was actually how you did it—at least, I hoped not. Our clinic was not much help, either: "You should really come into the doctor's office and let us handle it," said a wor-ried-sounding nurse when I asked for her input. So I looked up the at-home method online. Several independent websites detailed exactly what needed to be done. Of course, no two sites gave the same advice. Some recommend the use of an *actual* turkey baster, but those sites all looked worryingly amateurish, so I homed in on places that suggested using the needleless syringe method. Finding needleless syringes online was not easy, mainly because I had no idea what size we would need. I wanted the syringe to be long and thin, to look as close as possible to the one our doctor had used. But noth-ing I found online came close. It occurred to me that the market for a lesbian home-insemination kit was wide open for the taking.

Perplexed, I called Sarah. "Go downstairs to the drugstore in our building and ask the pharmacist," she said, sounding surprised that I perceived this as a dilemma. I'd grown so accustomed to handling all of our reproductive needs from the comfort of my desk chair that it never dawned on me to walk downstairs and speak with a live person working within the confines of my own apartment building.

But there was something underneath my apparent oblivious-ness to the world at large. I did not want to have to explain why I needed needleless syringes to someone face-to-face. I tried convincing myself that this was because what we were doing was a private matter. But I knew that wasn't why I was apprehensive.

After all the years of therapy, my struggle to come out and gain acceptance from family and friends, I still felt ashamed about my sexuality. If you'd asked me at that time in my life if I felt proud to be gay, I would have answered with a resounding yes. And if you'd asked how I felt about my relationship with Sarah, I would have insisted I wanted it to be as public as possible; after all, I adored her. But the truth was I'd performed night after night in packed houses, allowing fans to believe I might be straight. I'd done press interviews cautiously choosing my pronouns, referring to girlfriends as "my partner," "they," "them," "it"—anything to avoid using a female-defining word and being forced out of the closet. Now that I was embarking on one of the most common and universal human experiences, I could see that I wasn't going to be given the same free pass by society. It was time to face the truth.

I walked into the drugstore and sheepishly headed to the pharmacist's counter. I decided to give up as little information as possible and deal with my inner self-loathing afterward. "Do you have needleless syringes?" I asked the young girl manning the cash register.

"What size do you need?" she asked without looking up.

"Long and thin, preferably without a needle on the end of it," I responded.

This, of course, prompted the question "What do you need it for?"

"You don't want to know," I responded. She stared at me for a few seconds, then swiveled around to look for the syringes.

I felt a sense of relief that she was satisfied with my answer, but I was also filled with shame and remorse for not being able to say "I need it to get my partner pregnant tonight when she gets home from work, you nosy thing." Before I could drown in my own embarrassment, she returned with two syringes. They seemed like the right size, and I saw that the needles screwed off at the bottom. Perfect. "Do you have more than just two?" I asked.

"Sorry, that's all we have in stock," she responded. "That will be twelve cents."

Finally, I thought. A bargain. I walked home clutching the syringes, the spoils of victory, tightly in hand.

Sarah

Hailing a cab on the streets of New York with a three-foot-tall aluminum tank in your possession is no easy task. Neither is getting it past your doorman, especially one like ours. John took pride in knowing the name of every single one of the five hundred residents living in our building and he rarely missed an opportunity to greet each one as they passed by. To the untrained eye, I'm sure it looked more like we were making a bomb than a baby. Having contemplated several ways to sneak past him without being noticed, we decided that Kristen would play the decoy and approach his desk to discuss the "leak" in our apartment while I ran by hoisting a twenty-five-pound nitrogen tank. Then Kristen and I would meet back up in our apartment. Hopefully he wouldn't notice and call the FBI's Terrorism Task Force.

At ten thirty A.M., Kristen sauntered over to John with a look of consternation on her face. "There's a pool of water around the bathtub," I heard her saying as I dashed past the two of them, my arms wrapped around the tank.

"Maybe you took a bath and the water splashed on the floor?" John replied.

"Hmm, that's a good point," Kristen said.

I waited by the elevator, breathing hard. A neighbor from another floor, whom I recognized but didn't know, approached and gave me a polite smile. His eyes flickered from the tank to the elevator doors, and when they opened, he gestured for me to go ahead. Then he stepped back and waited for the doors to close. Okay, so maybe *he* was going to call the terrorist hotline; at least I'd gotten the damn thing into the elevator. The first part of Operation Home Insemination was successful. We now had a nitrogen tank good for seven days filled with three vials of our donor's specimen.

The second part of the plan was a bit more complicated; I had to ovulate. Peeing on a stick every morning now came with one new anxiety-ridden layer: the ticking tank of nitrous oxide filled with fifteen hundred dollars worth of donor specimen that sat in the hallway closet. Upon declaring we would try from home, I had stopped taking the fertility drugs that had regulated my cycle down to the minute. The first month off the drugs threw my system into a tailspin, and my ovulation was late—so late we had to pick up more nitrous oxide for our tank. Add another $250 to the tab.

With the weekend fast approaching, our mothers announced they'd be coming in to see us. One had show tickets and the other had firm plans to see friends, and our apartment was to serve as their personal headquarters. We now ran the risk of inseminating from home while both mothers were visiting. At that point, they knew I was on fertility drugs and were aware of the unsuccessful pregnancy attempts but had no idea we'd be trying from home that month. So they seemed mystified that their decision to "do New York City" was met with great resistance by us.

"I have theater tickets, you can just go about your business," my mother said when she called.

I hung up and laughed, "If only she knew what our *business* was!"

Kristen's mother wouldn't take no for an answer, either. When Kristen tried to argue our apartment wasn't that big, her mother said insistently, "I've been in that apartment and not only is it spacious, it's *gorgeous*. I'd invite my girlfriends to stay as well if they didn't already have hotel reservations!"

I relented. "Okay. We're excited you are coming, but we might not be totally available." It looked like we had lost the good fight.

The weekend would consist of us, our mothers, our cryo tank, and half a dozen ovulation tests.

That weekend Kristen and I guarded the hallway closet that held the tank like night watchmen. It seemed like every time one of us stepped out of the living room, another mother was nosing around the closet—first to hang a coat, then to take a coat, then to find a blanket or a sweater or a vacuum cleaner. At one point one mother gave her friend an actual tour of our closet to show off how impressively organized it was. She opened the door, pointing to our "clever" coat rack and our California Closet–like shelves, while the nitrogen tank stood nestled in plain sight. Unbelievably, it went completely undetected. On Sunday night, we kissed our mothers good-bye and said a prayer to the ovulation gods. And it worked! Monday morning arrived with a dark purple line. We were officially entering my optimum fertilization window. The operation was now in full effect.

That evening, after a candlelit dinner, Kristen and I pulled the cryogenic tank out of our closet. Smoke billowed from the top as we removed the lid.

"This is very Harry Potter–esque," I said.

"Or *Spinal Tap*," Kristen said with a giggle, peering into the top.

Pulling one small vial off the stem, we carefully placed the other vials back into the freezing-cold tank. We waited about forty-five minutes for the sample to thaw before we were finally ready to begin. We were both excited and doing everything we could to keep our nerves under control. The vial was so small you could easily lose control of it while unscrewing the top. Kristen reached for the syringe and tried to place it into the vial to draw our specimen out, but the syringe was too wide to fit into the vial. We could not get the newly thawed specimen out! Panic quickly replaced our feelings of excitement. Kristen threw on her flip-flops and tore out of the apartment. It was 8:55 P.M. and the pharmacy closed at 9:00 P.M.

Kristen

I ran around the corner only to find the pharmacy was already closed. A sob rose into my throat as I cupped my hands and peered into the window. Through the glass, I saw a man in a white jacket moving around in the dimly lit store. I started rattling the gate, then banging on it. Several minutes passed before he looked up. "Closed," he mouthed, then waved me away.

"It's an emergency!" I shouted, continuing to bang on the gate. Passersby were starting to stare, but I didn't care. I was going to rattle that cage until he let me in. Finally he walked toward the front of the store, shaking his head. He opened the door enough to hear me, but not enough for me to reach through. "I need a syringe with a narrow top," I exclaimed. A frown settled over his features as if he suspected I was a drug addict, and he started to close the door.

"No, you don't understand!" I shouted. "My partner is ovulating and I need to inseminate her! I've got five hundred dollars worth of thawed donor specimen in my living room and time is running out!" I didn't care who heard or what the pharmacist thought of me. I was thinking of Sarah—and our rapidly evaporating dream.

Something changed in his features. "One minute," he said, and went to the back of the store. He shortly reappeared with a handful of syringe options and unlocked the gate. I took a few of each kind, thanked him profusely, and handed him a ten dollar bill. He refused the money and wished me good luck. Then I raced back up to the apartment and began testing the syringes to see if any would fit. Sarah looked up at me as one of the needles slid seamlessly into the vial. We had a match.

Sarah

Ever since we started the insemination process, my life had become a waiting game divided into two-week cycles. Very few people at work knew what I was up to, so after each negative pregnancy result, I was forced to put on a happy face. Then I would have to wait two weeks before I could test to see if I was ovulating. Once I was, I would head over to the doctor's office for an insemination. It would then take two more weeks before I could take a pregnancy test. I could never wait that long. After only four days, I would run down to the drugstore to buy an early detection home pregnancy test. I'd pee on the stick, place it gingerly onto the sink, and then pace around my apartment. After five minutes that seemed like fifty, I would race back to the bathroom to check the results while holding my breath. And it would always be negative, causing a tidal wave of disappointment. When I showed the stick to Kristen, she would try to comfort me by saying, "It's still too early for the pregnancy hormone to be detected."

This became my tradition: Feel the devastation early, each and every month. After a few days passed, I would move through the devastation phase into denial, convinced the early negative was false and that I might still be pregnant. I'd wake up obsessed with one thing: peeing on a stick. I'd jump out of bed and rush over to the bathroom, take the test, and stare at the result so hard I could practically will two lines to show up. Inevitably, only one would appear. I would repeat this ritual each morning until I got my period. Then the cramps would start, depression would slowly set in, and the cycle would start over, month after month after month.

But the month we tried from home was different. I didn't waste my time on one of the early detection sticks; I couldn't bear another negative result. I waited until I was "late." On that Friday, I called Kristen from my office in the middle of the day. "I'm trying to play it cool, and that's why I haven't said anything, but I was supposed to get my period yesterday," I said.

"Are you sure?" she asked with excitement creeping into her voice.

"I'm positive, but my cycle could be totally screwed up because of all the Clomid I was on."

"Babe, this is sooo exciting—late is late," Kristen said insistently. "But let's give it a few more days, in case it *is* the aftereffects of the drugs."

I agreed, and we tried to contain our excitement. Two days later, I peed on the stick and crawled back into bed with *The New York Times,* a cup of coffee, and Kristen. We chatted while trying to forget about the stick sitting on our nightstand. After several minutes, I couldn't stand it anymore: I grabbed the stick and took a look. Exasperated, I said, "No line! Wait a minute . . ." If I tilted the stick a certain way, I could see the faintest hint of . . . something. I ran to the window and held it up directly to the light. *"I think I see a line!"* I yelled, handing the stick to Kristen to confirm my findings.

She held it one way, then another, and said, "I really don't see anything, babe." She then put it directly up to the sunlight. "Wait a second. *I think you're right!"*

We flagged a cab and headed straight to our doctor's office. On a weekend, the forty-block trip usually took ten minutes, but that morning, it felt more like an hour-and-a-half ride. Because it was Sunday, they weren't open for long. We had fifteen minutes to get there and give blood. We skidded through the doors with my pregnancy test in hand, wrote our names on the sign-in sheet, and took a seat. Moments later my name was called. I handed the nurse—a warm, gregarious woman I'd never seen before—my stick and asked her opinion. "If you see a line, it's a line," she said. "There's no such thing as a false positive when it comes to these sticks."

"I want to believe you," I said. "But do you see a line?"

"Uh-huh, I see it. It's faint, barely even there. But it's a line. That's a baby."

I still didn't believe her. I'd waited so long and experienced so much disappointment. I immediately put the thought out of my head and held out my arm for the nurse to draw my blood. She said she'd call later to confirm the results. Kristen and I headed straight home. Just as we pushed the front door open, my phone rang. It was the nurse from the office. "Sarah?" she said. "Congratulations!"

I looked at Kristen and shouted, "We're pregnant!"

She repeated the same words over and over as we jumped up and down and hugged. "We're pregnant, we're pregnant!" she cried.

We spent the rest of the day at home, ordering in and watching TV. We didn't call our mothers or any of our friends—not yet, anyway. We wanted a day to bask in our new status of moms-to-be. Finally, we were going to be a family.

Chapter 6

This Is How a Heart Breaks

Sarah

On November 27, 2007, I turned thirty-six years old. I was four weeks pregnant and already showing signs. Since the blood test had confirmed the good news, I couldn't wait to share it with the people I loved. I could finally tell my mother about the night she'd almost stumbled across the tank in the closet! My parents drove into the city to take Kristen and me to our favorite restaurant, a Venetian trattoria called Le Zie.

"You look beautiful!" my mom exclaimed as we settled into a red leather banquette.

"Thanks," I said, though I didn't feel beautiful. I was battling nausea and fatigue so acute that when I sat down at the table, I couldn't decide if I should face-plant or vomit. I reached for the breadbasket as a waiter approached, in the hopes that a small bite would calm my stomach.

"What can I bring you to drink?" he asked.

"Just a glass of water, I'm not feeling so hot," I said.

"I wouldn't have come into the city if I'd known you weren't feeling well," my mother said, lowering her reading glasses onto her nose and peering at the menu. "I'll have a glass of merlot." Then she turned to me. "I have a present for you—something special for your thirty-sixth birthday." She reached into her bag and drew out a long, wrapped box. "This was your grandmother's, then mine—now it's yours," she said. I untied the ribbon and opened the box. Nestled in tissue was a thick sterling silver necklace with a large silver oval pendant.

"It's beautiful, I love it!" I exclaimed as she fastened it around my neck.

"It's gorgeous," Kristen said, and gave me a knowing smile.

"Actually, we have a present for you, too," I said.

Before I could continue, my mother looked at Kristen, then at me, and then threw her arms around my neck and cried, "You're pregnant!" Then she burst into tears.

My father smiled in his stoic way; I could tell he was beaming. "Congratulations, Sass," he said, calling me by the nickname he'd given me as a child. He put an arm around Kristen, squeezed her shoulder, and joked, "Millions of dollars in doctor's fees, and you were the one to finally get her pregnant!"

"Who can I tell?" my mother asked, ticking off a list of names. "Does your brother know yet? I need to call Aunt Anne . . ."

"Now, Mom, I am *just* pregnant," I said cautiously. "I wouldn't tell anyone yet. We're telling both sets of parents. That's it!" But there was no stopping my mother. That night, she got out her tattered Filofax and systematically went through the alphabet; by the time she was finished, everyone she'd ever met had been informed she was going to be a grandmother.

"I don't know if that was such a great idea," Kristen said as we were getting ready for bed that night.

"Forget about it—this is my mother we're talking about," I responded. "When she gets an idea in her head, there's no stopping her."

"I always wondered where you got that from," Kristen said,

laughing as I playfully smacked her in the arm. I climbed into bed and snuggled up to her as the lights of the Empire State Building went dark. I could think of no better way to start my thirty-sixth year.

Earlier that fall, Kristen and I had bought a weekend home in Sea Cliff, New York—an eclectic enclave on Long Island, right next to the town Kristen had grown up in. At the same time, our lease was ending on our place in the city, so we moved into a studio apartment we'd purchased on West Fifteenth Street in Manhattan. With a baby on the way, we were done renting; we wanted to invest in our future, as a family. We would spend weekends at the beach and weekdays in the city. Kristen organized the movers and packed every box; I wasn't allowed to lift a finger. I enjoyed playing the pregnancy card, sitting with my feet up and reading magazines as Kristen catered to my every whim. Our new apartment was small, but bright and sunny, and located in a prime area of New York City. Plus, with the purchase of the Sea Cliff house, we had a place to stretch out and store things. I no longer felt like we were playing house. Now we were actually living it.

It's a Henderson family tradition to spend Christmas Eve together at Kristen's parents' house in Glen Cove, New York. We had already told her mother and father our big news, and now we were ready to share it with her enormous extended family. But we didn't want to make a grand statement. Instead, we hoped the news would trickle from person to person. As eggnogs were being poured, Kristen's theatrical younger cousin, Matt, noticed the fact that I refused a glass. Matt's histrionic reaction raised suspicion around the room: Cupping his hands around his mouth, he shouted at me, "Are you pregnant?"

Kristen's cousin Kelly whipped her head around. "Who's pregnant?" she asked, then pointed an accusing finger at Kristen's sister-in-law, Klio. "Is it you?"

"I'm not pregnant," Klio said. "At least I'd better not be!"

"What? Who's pregnant?" cried Kristen's aunt Ro, jumping to her feet with excitement. So much for our dream of a quiet announcement. It was more like a game of Telephone, played out on the Jumbotron at a football game.

"Hey, everybody, it's me!" I announced, waving my hands in the air. "I'm the one who's pregnant. We'd hoped to tell each of you individually, but anyway . . . there's a new Hendo grandbaby on the way!" The family swarmed around us as I proudly showed off my belly.

As the weeks wore on, I walked around repeatedly checking my belly in the mirror to see if it had grown. And indeed, I did start to show earlier than most women. By late December, I'd bought my first pair of maternity jeans. "Hot," Kristen said as I snapped the elastic waistband into place. Every time Kristen walked through the door, she was carrying another armload of books: *What to Expect When You're Expecting*, *Spiritual Midwifery*, *Great Expectations: Your All-in-One Resource for Pregnancy and Childbirth*. We kept a photo album of sonograms and started to debate names. My pregnancy was all we talked about.

At work, I told no one but my two closest friends, which made dealing with morning sickness—or, as I would call it, "round-the-clock sickness"—harder to hide. I never actually threw up, but I never felt well; nausea was my constant companion. I also had a horrible metallic taste in my mouth, so I spent all day sucking Jolly Ranchers. Each morning when I woke up, I thought about only one thing: going to bed at night.

"Your hormones are making you sick, which means your body is doing exactly what it's supposed to be doing," said Kristen, pointing to a section she'd found in one of the books. As awful as I felt, I had to admit I found comfort in the nausea because it meant the pregnancy was going well. And indeed, right on schedule, the doctor detected a heartbeat at my eight-week sonogram. It seemed all of my heartache was finally behind me.

Late in my first trimester, I left for Dallas on a business trip. I was traveling there to pitch our biggest program of the year to one of our most important clients. A week before the trip, I checked in with Dr. Rosenbaum, my ob-gyn, to get the all-clear. "Your first trimester has gone smoothly, so I see no reason why you shouldn't," she said. I was relieved; it wasn't part of my makeup to refuse a business trip. And I certainly didn't want to have to come up with an explanation for why I was staying home.

The day of the trip, I boarded the plane with my coworker Karen. She didn't know I was pregnant, though she may have suspected a food addiction since I was starting to bust out of all of my clothes. I had to pee halfway through the flight, so I excused myself and squeezed into the tiny bathroom. As I lowered my pants and underwear, I froze. Small, dark spots dotted my underwear. I rubbed the fabric between my thumb and forefinger; yep, the substance was unmistakably blood. I started to panic as I ran through possible explanations in my head. Hadn't Kristen read something to me about spotting in *What to Expect When You're Expecting*? Well, I certainly didn't expect *this*. Not at thirty thousand feet, hurtling toward Dallas with no high-tech medical equipment in sight. "This isn't good," I murmured as I washed my hands and made my way back up the aisle.

Karen was sitting next to the window with her headphones on, engrossed in an issue of *People*. "Can I tell you something?" I asked.

She took her ear buds out and lowered the magazine to her lap. "Yeah, sure. You okay?"

I must have looked pale with shock. "Well, no," I admitted. My eyes filled with tears. "I'm eleven weeks pregnant and bleeding. I'm *freaking out*."

"Oh, honey," she said, taking my hand. "Do *not* worry—I've definitely heard of spotting and I'm sure you're okay." Karen was the mother of three children herself, so I found her words comforting.

Still, I wished she'd said, "I spotted through all three pregnancies—it's nothing!"

As soon as the plane's wheels touched the tarmac in Texas, I fumbled for my phone and called Dr. Rosenbaum. By then, I had her on speed-dial. "It's perfectly normal to spot during the first trimester," she said, trying to reassure me. "The flight likely caused a shift in your body; do not worry. But you should probably try to get home." Hearing her calm, level voice *was* comforting, but I still felt something wasn't right.

When I calmed down, I called my mother to bring her into the loop. "What does the doctor say?" she asked, alarmed.

"She said I should elevate my legs when I get to the hotel room," I said. "And to try to get home. But if nothing changes, I'll probably stay for the meeting. I'm flying home tomorrow afternoon anyway."

"When will you get to the room? Do you need me to fly out there?"

"No, Mom, thank you, I'm going to be fine. Really. I have to call Kristen."

As I told Kristen the news, I could sense her distress. I could tell she was trying to hold it together for my sake. "Everything is going to be fine," I said firmly, though I didn't feel remotely confident about that statement.

"I love you, baby," she responded, her voice cracking. "Put your feet up and call me back."

Karen and I continued on to the hotel and checked into our separate rooms. I did just what the doctor told me to do, stacking three pillows under my knees and spending the rest of the night prone on the king-sized bed, staring blankly at *Dancing with the Stars*. At eleven P.M. I went to the bathroom and peered nervously into my underwear. What had looked like a few drops of blood before was now a bright red polka-dot pattern. "There's nothing you can do about it, so go to sleep," I told myself, grabbing a new pair of underwear from my suitcase and unwrapping one of the panty liners I'd bought at the hotel shop. Then I climbed into bed. Hugging my pillow, I prayed for the best. "Please, God, help me," I whispered as tears started to stream down my cheeks. "I want this baby so badly." I didn't know what else to say. I had never felt so alone.

In the morning, I emitted a strangled sob when I saw that the panty liner was soaked through and blood ran in thin rivulets down the insides of my thighs. My finger shaking, I dialed my boss. "I think I might be having a miscarriage; I'm going to need to skip the meeting," I said, trying to hold my voice steady.

"I'm so sorry, get on a plane and *come home*," he said insistently.

With every call to my mother, I could hear her devastation growing deeper and deeper. "I'm headed to the airport right now," I promised. By the time I landed in New York, I was doubled over with cramps. I stumbled to the town car that had arrived to pick me up and curled up in the backseat, clutching my stomach. My voice was barely audible as I gave the driver my address. "Please hurry," I whispered.

As I stared at the back of the leather seat in front of me, my thoughts drifted to my mother. At sixty-eight years old, she was having health problems. The idea of losing her was unimaginable to me and gave rise to a crystal-clear thought: I can't have her die without her knowing my baby. I knew my mother wanted to be alive for those grandchildren I was going to give her. But all that was forced into the background of my thoughts by the immediate pain I was feeling in my midsection.

As soon as I arrived home, Kristen yanked open the door of the car and took my suitcase from the driver. Offering her arm for support, she gingerly led me upstairs, where we dropped off my things before rushing back out to Dr. Rosenbaum's office. For the sixth time in three months, I changed into a paper gown and climbed onto the cold metal table for a sonogram. This time, though, Sheila the technician's expression was grim. She squeezed a dollop of jelly onto my stomach, then rolled the scanner over it, pressing into my abdomen to get a better look. Kristen gripped my hand, squinting at the screen in the hopes of seeing that delicate and fragile heartbeat we'd come to depend on. Finally, Sheila placed the scanner on a tray and rolled her chair back a few inches from the examination table. "I'm so sorry," she said, growing misty-eyed. "I know how much this meant to you both."

Eleven weeks into my pregnancy and it was over. Just like that. Kristen cried so hard no sound escaped her; she just shook. Sheila withdrew quietly from the room to give us some time alone. After five minutes, I gently shook Kristen's shoulder and told her that I had to call my mom. The conversation with my mother turned out to be no easier: She kept saying, "Oh, Sarah, I'm so sorry. I'm just so sorry." I could hear her trying to hold back the tears. This was a woman who could see the silver lining in anything—and yet she couldn't find one here. It was the first time I'd seen her visibly upset since her father had passed away. "What did the doctor say?" she finally managed to ask. "Do you need a D and C?" A "dilation and curettage" is a surgical procedure designed to clean out the uterus after a miscarriage. Thankfully, I'd been told I probably wouldn't need one.

"No, Mom, the doctor says it'll pass at some point in the next few days. We're just going to go home and be on our own."

"Okay," she sniffled, and got off the phone. She now had to break the news to everyone she'd told about the pregnancy, while I headed home to face all the pregnancy paraphernalia we no longer needed.

Once back in our apartment, Kristen set me up on the couch with a blanket and pillows. We ordered in and spent the day watching bad TV. Kristen kept falling into long crying jags. "Why did this happen to that little soul?" she asked again and again. Hearing her plaintive cries broke my heart. Bleary-eyed and spent, I fell asleep in her lap, periodically waking up to intense waves of cramps. Kristen kept running to the closet to grab fresh towels to spread underneath me, to make sure the blood didn't reach the couch.

At nine P.M., I wobbled into the bathroom to change my maxi-pad. When I sat down on the toilet, I felt a large clump pass between my legs. "Oh! Kris, I think it just happened," I called out in a shaky voice.

Kristen appeared in the doorway, her face blotchy and red. "Where?" she asked.

"There," I said, pointing into the toilet. A red, gelatinous mass was suspended in the water; it wasn't uterine lining. "Do I flush?" I asked, my face contorted with horror.

Kristen nodded. "I—I guess so."

I flushed and covered my face with my hands. We'd felt the heart-break keenly ever since the sonogram, but this moment made it so final; we were devastated.

I continued to bleed through the night and stayed home from work the next day. When I awoke that morning, Kristen, who'd barely slept at all, was sitting up staring at me. "I was watching you in case you had a bad dream," she said, rubbing her swollen eyes.

"Thanks," I replied sadly.

"The book said that sometimes this happens when there's something wrong with the baby and that this is nature's way of correcting itself," she said, leaning over to the windowsill to grab a tissue. "That's supposed to make us feel better." She sobbed the words into her tissue.

"Maybe," I said as I swung my legs to the floor and started to get up to pour myself a bowl of cereal.

Kristen suddenly sprang to life. "Don't—I'll get that."

"Okay," I said, sinking back into the couch amid the towels and balled-up tissues.

"As soon as you're ready to try again, we'll get right back on it," Kristen said as she prepared my breakfast in our tiny kitchen.

"Mmm-hmm."

"Maybe we should look at IVF," I said. Kristen paused to place a bowl of cereal and a glass of orange juice in front of me.

Taking an inordinately long period of time to arrange my spoon and napkin, she finally said, "If you're having problems, shouldn't I try, too?"

My brain felt foggy. "I don't know," I said. "I don't know. I don't know what to do."

Sensing my spiral, Kristen dropped the conversation. "Everything happens for a reason," she said. "We'll get through this."

After only one day off, I decided to head back to work. "You can stay home longer," Kristen said.

"What am I going to do here—lie on the couch and feel depressed?" I responded. I felt as though I had failed her, my mother, and worst of all, myself. At work, I had the grim task of facing the people I had already told. I was lucky to work in a supportive environment, but I still found the conversations sad, uncomfortable, and embarrassing. In most cases, I felt compelled to manage *their* reactions: "I'm fine, really," I found myself saying, though it was the farthest thing from the truth.

If I couldn't imagine ever feeling better, Kristen was in even worse shape. Most nights I would come home to find her sitting on the bed, watching TV with a tearstained face. One night, while she was unable to stop crying on the phone, her mother told her, "You know, the doctors thought I lost a twin while I was pregnant with your brother. I had a similar experience as Sarah, but somehow I remained pregnant. They couldn't tell for sure back then, but I always assumed I lost your brother's twin. And I know this seems hard to believe right now, but time does heal all wounds." Her mother's words were comforting, but we felt time was our enemy. The days were long and the nights unrelenting. My physical recuperation dragged on as long as my emotional one. At thirty-six, my body was not as quick to bounce back as it had been in the past, and several months passed before I had a normal menstrual cycle.

Then I found my first ray of hope. One day, Kristen and I were walking by a pet store a few blocks away from our apartment when I noticed a puppy sleeping in the window. He weighed no more than three pounds and had champagne-colored fur; the sign said he was a cockapoo. I joined a knot of women gathered around the glass, cooing over him. I couldn't resist ducking inside to get a better look. "Honey, you are crazy, we are not getting a puppy," Kristen said, tugging at my arm. I refused to allow her to drag me away. A pet store employee lifted the puppy's warm, floppy body from the window and put him down on his wobbly feet at the back of the store.

"He's so cute!" I cried as I fawned over him.

Kristen had to agree. By the time he crawled into my lap and snuggled up against my stomach, I had taken out my credit card. It was ironic: While Kristen had always wanted a dog, I'd always resisted bringing one home. I had my sights set on a baby, not a puppy. Now I needed that three-pound ball of unconditional love. Kristen named him Tucker before the cashier could crate him and send us on our way. All the love we'd reserved for the baby we'd just lost was transferred to him—and he gladly accepted it. When we got him home, Kristen looked through his paperwork and saw his birth date: January 7. The color drained from her face. "Sarah," she whimpered, pushing his papers toward me. "Look at his birth date. It's the exact same day you miscarried." Very rarely did I get on board with Kristen's synchronistic theories, but I couldn't deny this one. "Clearly, he was meant to be ours," I said, cradling him.

Tucker was served only the best foods, slept in a monogrammed dog bed, and was sent to puppy kindergarten, where he graduated at the top of his class. Kristen took him on long walks and play-dates at the dog run. Gigi would come visit after school and play fetch with him in the hallway. Our mothers referred to Tucker as their "grand-puppy." He healed the whole family.

Chapter 7

The Power of Two

Sarah

In February of 2008, Kristen went out on a weeklong tour. As usual, the day before she left, our apartment was an explosion of clothes and instruments. I helped her pack and carry her suitcases downstairs. Then I kissed her good-bye and watched the taxi pull away. I let myself into the apartment and bent down to pet Tucker, who was dropping a ball at my feet. "Easy, boy, I can't play as hard as your other mother; it's just us for a little while," I said. I often felt melancholy when Kristen left on tour, but this time it was different. Tucker crawled into my lap and fell asleep. I was no longer alone.

The next night, Kristen called me from Philadelphia. "How are you, baby?" she asked. "How's Tucker?"

"We're good," I said, pulling his scrabbling body away from the shoe he was trying to destroy. "Tucker, *no!*" I said, admonishing him.

"Oh, good, sounds like business as usual," Kristen laughed. "How was the show?"

"Completely sold out, so there's that, at least. Listen, Sar . . ." She paused. "I'm feeling good now. Much better, actually. And I really am ready to start trying to get pregnant. To be honest, I don't want to wait another minute, much less another month."

"You're right—it is a good idea," I said, and meant it. Kristen was a year older than I was and hadn't even started to undergo fertility tests. We were no longer naïve about how long it might take to get pregnant. "Let's have you try at home, during your next cycle. We'll try at the same time. One of us is bound to end up pregnant, right?"

"I love you," she said.

"I love you too," I responded. I couldn't share with Kristen my conflicted feelings about our new plan. Deep down, I was terrified she would get pregnant before I did. I already felt like I'd lost a child in Gigi; then I'd lost a baby, now I was going to lose my dream of being pregnant. Like the bridesmaid who watches her friends get married one by one, I felt like I was surrounded by something that could never be mine. But the thought was so unfair to Kristen—and so in opposition to our common goal—that I pushed it to the very bottom of my psyche, where I hoped it would fade away.

Kristen returned from tour just as she was about to ovulate. Fortunately, we were old pros with the at-home method, so on Oscar night in 2008—exactly one year since I had started trying—we prepared ourselves for our monthly ritual, only this time our roles were reversed. Then we began the familiar waiting game. Two weeks later, with one negative result officially under her belt, Kristen decided to make a trip to the doctor. The appointment confirmed what we both had feared. Her FSH numbers were elevated, which meant there were issues with the quality and number of her reproductive eggs. The doctor recommended she start a round of Clomid, the same fertility drug I had taken.

Kristen was still deeply affected by the miscarriage I had suffered two months earlier, so the news that she could potentially have trouble conceiving came as a crushing blow. Despite her prior trepidation regarding medical intervention, she was now ready to do anything the doctors recommended. She willingly started taking the dreaded Clomid, determined to change our fortunes and provide us with the baby we both longed for. But it didn't take long for Clomid to alter my once mellow and optimistic partner into a stressed-out and high-strung woman. As I walked off the elevator toward our apartment one night, I heard my neighbor screaming at the top of her lungs. Shocked by the profanity she was using, I stopped dead in my tracks, only to realize the voice I heard was actually Kristen's. As I opened our apartment door, I found Kristen pacing back and forth, the phone held to her ear with one hand, the other waving the Discover card bill in the air. "I'll hold all day while you get your goddamned manager on the line," she shrieked. "I don't give a shit. I've been a customer for over ten years and will not tolerate being scammed by your fucking company another minute!" Veins were bulging in her neck and forehead. The solid foundation I had come to depend on was crumbling, just when I needed it most.

I had attended a charity auction around the same time I bought Tucker. I desperately needed a distraction from the yearlong roller coaster we'd been on, so I threw out a bid on a five-day trip to Italy, scheduled to take place in late April 2008. Much to my surprise, I won. I spent the week in Rome with Kristen eating, drinking, and taking in the sights. At night, I dreamed about a future trip to Europe with our young family in tow. Kristen, on the other hand, spent the entire vacation in a Clomid-induced haze, obsessed with the timing of her next ovulation. Even as we pulled up to the famed Colosseum in a tour bus and watched it rise majestically over the city, Kristen was whispering in a worried voice, "Are you *sure* we'll be home in time for my next cycle?"

Before taking Clomid, Kristen had sworn we would not let our pregnancy efforts rule our lives. But now, with the fertility treatment wreaking havoc on her body, she felt differently. The drug caused her cycle to fluctuate several days in either direction, so we had no idea when she would start ovulating. If it happened while we were in Italy, we would never make it back to the States in time.

She would be forced to sit out that month and remain on the fertility drug for another four weeks. She tried her best to enjoy the vacation, but fears about her cycle lurked behind every palazzo, every bite of gelato. Soon, I too was counting the days until we could leave.

Hours before our flight home, Kristen took an ovulation detection test. The result was positive. Instantly, she became a woman possessed, flying around our hotel room, throwing clothes into bags. "Kris—*Kris*—there is no reason to stress like that—it's not going to make our flight leave any sooner!" I exclaimed. The entire flight home, Kristen jiggled her legs, opened and closed magazines, and fiddled with the button for the overhead light. As soon as we landed at JFK we jumped into a cab and headed straight to the doctor's office. A routine exam concluded Kristen had three viable eggs for insemination. The doctor administered a shot of HCG, a drug that induces ovulation within twenty-four hours, and we returned on the following two mornings for intrauterine insemination, or IUI, procedures.

There was no time to get anxious waiting for Kristen's results. The day she had her second IUI procedure, a package arrived on our doorstep for me, filled with several different fertility medications. I had told Dr. Mattingly that I was willing to try an IVF cycle, but I was not sure when I wanted to start. Now the medications were in my possession: Some were time-sensitive, and none were cheap. "Now or never," I said to myself as I placed the bottles in the refrigerator, one by one.

A few months earlier, Kristen and I had taken a class that explained the various medications and how to administer the shots. Neither of us had ever given ourselves or anyone else a shot with a hypodermic needle. When the instructor had gone through the steps, we'd looked at each other with horror. "There will be several weeks of self-induced shots to your stomach; then you'll administer inch-and-a-half-long needles to the buttocks, followed by a perfectly timed dose of Lupron—which you'll have to place precisely two inches lower on your buttocks than any prior shot you've given yourself, or we can't retrieve your eggs properly," the instructor said, droning on and on. We were so overwhelmed and confused by the end of the session that we declared that neither of us would ever be willing to do an IVF cycle. Yet here we were, staring at what seemed to be hundreds of glass medication vials on the shelf of our refrigerator. I knew that if I couldn't make a baby with the contents of these vials, I couldn't make a baby at all.

Two weeks later I started my first IVF cycle. Kristen pulled up a website tutorial on administering the medications and we watched it together. When we finished, we debated some of the possible things that could go wrong: "What if you jab me and *miss?*" I asked fearfully.

"I'm more worried about spilling this stuff," Kristen admitted. "It's more expensive than liquid gold."

"What if you hit a vein or one of my organs?" I said. I couldn't stop coming up with scary scenarios. It just didn't seem responsible to have two people with no medical background administer all these medications.

Of course, there was one thing we'd never before discussed—the possibility of both of us getting pregnant at the same time. Sure, it had crossed my mind once or twice—the thought certainly made me nervous—but I had grown so pessimistic about the process, the idea seemed ludicrous. When I mentioned it to Kristen in passing, she was downright excited by the prospect.

"I *hope* it happens!" she exclaimed as I drew the medicine out of the bottle with a syringe.

"Would you mind not making jokes like that right this minute?" I asked. I was standing in front of her, holding my T-shirt up in order to expose my stomach.

"Sorry," she said.

I took a deep breath. "Okay, one . . . two . . . three!" I sucked in a great gulp of air and jabbed myself. "Ow!" I cried reflexively, grabbing for a cotton swab to wipe down the injection site. "Actually, it didn't hurt that much," I admitted. "I'm pretty good at this, considering that I am scared to death of needles. If my job in magazines doesn't work out, maybe I have a future in nursing."

"Ha ha," Kristen said. "Well, *you're* going to have to be good at this, because I'm not administering injections unless forced at gunpoint," she said. "I hate needles more than I hate clowns. Not to mention I'm busy over here trying to get pregnant myself."

Later that day, we got a call from the fertility clinic letting us know that Kristen's latest IUI had not produced a pregnancy. "Well, I guess we don't need to worry about being pregnant at the same time," I said when she got off the phone.

Kristen sighed. "Guess not."

We didn't have much time to dwell on our disappointment, though—we'd effectively entered the Amazing Race of Pregnancy. Kristen would run out to get a blood test while I watched an online tutorial; she would pop Clomid while I conjured up the courage to give myself a shot. My IVF cycle was intense and time-consuming. I had to follow very specific instructions for each medication: Some lasted only a few days, others for a few weeks. Some nights called for multiple shots; each came with online video tutorials I needed to watch. This busy schedule gave me hope. I finally felt like we were being proactive. The biggest obstacle was the long needles that Kristen had to inject into my butt at odd hours of the night. Every time we had to administer one of those shots in the two months leading up to the egg transfer, I would enter the bathroom, needle in hand, trembling and fighting nausea. Finally, I would call out to Kristen, "I'm ready!" The conversation would go something like this:

Me: "Ninety-nine, ninety-eight, ninety-seven, ninety-six . . . can you do this? I can't do this! "

Kristen: "Oh God, you really need *me* to do this for you? Can't we call Maura?" My sister-in-law, Maura, was a pediatric nurse at NYU hospital, only a few blocks from our apartment. She had offered to help with injections if I needed it. Unfortunately, it was one A.M. and she was not on duty.

"Egads, I have to stick this in your butt?" she gasped. "It's *really* long!"

Not exactly a confidence booster.

"I'm scared," I said. "Is this going to hurt?"

"I have no idea," she said. "I'm not trained to do this . . . Okay, it's done. How'd I do?"

"It's done? You did it? I don't even think I felt that—you're amazing! How did you do that?"

"I have absolutely no idea. See you tomorrow night."

After Kristen's latest negative pregnancy result, the doctor planned a procedure called an HSG. It was a test that would detect the health of her fallopian tubes by filling them with dye, a substance that would also clear any blockages within her tubes. Her HSG was scheduled for Tuesday, May 21, a date that fell exactly six days after her most recent period. At that point, I was well into my IVF cycle and getting ready for my own invasive egg-retrieval procedure. Mine, too, had to be scheduled on a very specific date: Tuesday, May 21. How we didn't see what the universe was planning for us at that moment, I don't know. A year and a half of negative results followed by a devastating miscarriage had convinced us that if just *one* of us could get pregnant, we would be so lucky. We just hoped it was a dream still within reach.

Kristen

The early part of 2008 was not only a stressful time personally, it was also a very hard time professionally. My band was doing short, sporadic tours in order to earn money while we waited for Starbucks to release our new CD. Unfortunately, the company was in the process of closing six hundred store locations nationwide, and Antigone Ris-

ing was not their top priority. Our attendance numbers were stag-
nant because we were hitting the same markets over and over with
no new CD to promote. Money was tight, and it was causing tension within the band.

So when the clinic told me that my FSH numbers were elevated,
they might as well have told me I had cancer. I was that devastated—
and *petrified* of having a miscarriage of my own. The day after I
found out, I shared a train ride with Cassidy from New York City to
Long Island. We were performing in a venue called the Crazy Don-
key—an apt name, considering how I felt that day. While I looked
out the window and worried about ever being able to have children,
Cassidy talked about her upcoming audition for a Broadway show.
It fell on the same day as a gig the band had been confirmed to do—
and we really needed the money.

She decided to go on the audition, causing the band to cancel the
date with little notice. I understood her desire to try something new,
it just could not have come at a worse time. Her decision to choose
an audition over a confirmed show only added to an already volatile
dynamic within the group. "Maybe we should all take a break from
relying on the band for money and find side gigs to help supplement
our incomes," I suggested. "That would give you an opportunity
to explore Broadway auditions while I start trying to get pregnant."
Cassidy didn't give a firm answer either way, and I couldn't blame
her. We'd worked so hard building Antigone Rising. I assumed the
thought of taking a break from it was a lot to take in. She just looked
ahead as the train chugged along. After that night's show, we played
again on Saturday night in Boston, Massachusetts. The following
day, Cassidy e-mailed our management to let them know that she
was not going to play any more shows; she was quitting the band.
Scheduled to leave two days later for a four-week tour, we were
forced to cancel the entire run of shows.

And yet I was in total denial about what was happening to the
band I loved. We were booked to play the Michigan Womyn's Music

Festival in August and I told my management not to cancel it. I figured she'd be back with the band by then.

I would say things like, "When she's ready to play again . . ."

And my management kept saying, "She won't be." I had spent the past ten years touring relentlessly with the band, always putting it first. My instinct was to get everyone together in a room, to work things out. But I was just starting to take Clomid; I needed to take care of myself for a change. I was done trying to mend fences between my bandmates. If we were meant to be together, she'd return on her own.

Despite its side effects, I popped Clomid like candy. "You've gone from Ms. Homegrown to 'Get me Dr. Mattingly—stat!'" laughed Sarah. "I love it." On the Tuesday of our scheduled procedures, we woke up early and ate breakfast together, since our appointments were in two different locations.

"Good luck," Sarah said as she headed out the door.

"Break an egg!" I shouted after her.

"Very funny," she retorted, and disappeared into the elevator.

Lenox Hill Hospital was the only place that could perform my HSG procedure on that date. I had an afternoon appointment, but when I arrived, the nurse at the front desk could not find me in the system. Naturally, there'd been a mix-up between the two doctors' offices. After ninety long minutes filled with several phone calls and faxes between the two offices, the confusion was finally cleared up and I was taken in for the exam.

"You may experience slight cramping as we inject the dye," the radiologist warned me. "It shouldn't be too bad. But just in case, you do have someone in the waiting room to help get you home, right?"

"Yeah," I lied.

How bad could it be? I thought. I'm in New York City; I'll just hop in a cab and be home in five minutes.

"Okay, we're starting the injection," the radiologist said.

Within seconds I was doubled over in pain. I felt nauseous and woozy and was experiencing intense cramps. "This is *way* worse than what you said," I moaned, leaning over the bucket she'd brought to the table in case I vomited.

"Yeah, sometimes people say that," she said as she packed up her instruments. "But there's someone in the waiting room for you, right? Lie here for a few minutes; I'll get you some maxi-pads. You'll bleed like you're having a light period for a day or two, but it's nothing to worry about. Then I'll send the pictures we got to your doctor. Sound good?" And she was off.

I rolled myself into the fetal position and tried to focus on the wall to make the room stop spinning. A few minutes later I stumbled off the table, got myself dressed, and slowly walked out of the hospital. It was raining and my ninety-minute wait had landed me right in the middle of rush hour in New York City. There were no cabs to be found.

The subway platform was packed with commuters. The cramping was getting worse and I could feel the bleeding getting heavier. I staggered over to some free space on the wall and propped myself against it. I pulled the hood of my jacket on and stood there, swaying, barely able to open my eyes. People were intentionally steering clear of me. I needed an express train but settled for a local when it arrived first. Squeezing into the crowded train, I allowed the surrounding bodies to hold me up. Eight stops later, the conductor's voice squawked, "Next stop, Union Square." The doors opened and spit me out onto the platform. I staggered through the turnstile, up the stairs, and across Fourteenth Street. By the time I put the key into the door of my apartment, I was sobbing and in need of assistance. As soon as I crossed the threshold, I lay down on the rug. Sarah was already in bed, doubled over in pain from her own procedure. Unable to get up to help me, she looked at me and we started to laugh uncontrollably. "Whose brilliant idea was this?" I muttered from the floor.

Sarah

When I arrived at the doctor's office for my procedure, I was led to an exam room and instructed to change into a gown. Shortly after, the doctor entered the room, holding a clipboard. "We're going to put you in a state called 'twilight'—which is general anesthesia, but it's not a deep sleep—then we use a laparoscope to go in and retrieve the eggs," he explained. "Once we're done, you'll rest in the recovery room for a half hour or so, and we'll definitely want you to drink a lot of fluids. Then I'll come back to check on you and let you know how many follicles we retrieved. At that point, whoever is here with you can take you home. You might have some light cramping and bleeding but otherwise it's pretty noninvasive. Any questions?"

I had lots of them but was more interested in getting the procedure over with, so I answered, "None. Let's do this."

When I came to in the recovery room, my first thought was, How can a male doctor know what "light cramping" feels like? Because this is *not* light cramping. When the doctor walked into the room, I was lying on my back, holding my stomach and moaning.

"Hi, Sarah, you did excellently," he said. "We have some healthy and viable follicles, which we're going to inseminate. We'll watch them over the course of the next few days to see how they develop, then the nurse will call you to schedule your transfer. And you don't have to be put under for that."

"Thank God," I mumbled.

He continued. "Now I just need you to drink a few glasses of water. Who's here to pick you up?"

"My partner, Kristen," I lied.

"Would you like the nurse to bring her in?" he asked.

"N-no, no, I'm fine," I stammered. "I just really need the water." I drank my water, changed back into my clothes, and whisked myself out of there as quickly as any woman experiencing horrible cramps could. The gods must have been with me, because when I got to the street there was a cab waiting right outside. I sank into the backseat and closed my eyes as the driver took me home.

Three days later, I got a call from Nurse Jan. "We'd like to wait until day five to transfer the embryos back inside of you," she said.

"My embryos don't look good?" I asked, terrified.

"No, Sarah, it's just the opposite," she responded. "Your embryos look so good we will have a difficult time deciding which ones to implant. If we give them a few days to mature, certain embryos will rise to the top, which will make our selection process easier."

"So everything is totally fine?" I asked in a voice that made it clear it would be impossible to reassure me enough. "You had no trouble inseminating my eggs and they are progressing as they should be?"

"Everything is totally fine," she said. "We will see you Monday afternoon." I shouted the news to Kristen, who was due to ovulate any day and was in the bathroom peeing on a stick. She emerged from the bathroom waving the stick in her hand. "It's positive. I have a feeling Monday morning could be the perfect storm."

Kristen

On Friday of Memorial Day weekend in 2008, the four remaining members of Antigone Rising met for the first time since Cassidy had quit the band nearly three months earlier. We were sitting on our drummer Dena's deck in New Jersey, talking about all we'd been through together as a band. "We've worked too long and too hard to throw away everything we've built together," said Cathy. We all agreed. We wanted to keep playing music together. Cathy told us she'd been contacted by the promoter of a Long Island festival; he wanted us to be the headline act. He knew our situation, but he loved the band and wanted us to play as a foursome. Rehearsals would start the following week. I knew that I was going to be ovulating in the next few days and could possibly be pregnant by the time our rehearsals began, but I did not want to share this with my bandmates just yet. We'd all been through enough in the past few months. I couldn't throw another monkey wrench into our plans. So I kept quiet about what Sarah and I would be doing that weekend.

Sarah

Kristen and I were both due at the fertility clinic on Memorial Day. The streets of New York City were empty, as most of its residents had packed up and gone to the beach. Not us. We were still there, like lone survivors of a nuclear blast. We arrived at the office first thing that morning, took our seats in the uncharacteristically empty waiting room, and listened patiently for Kristen's name to be called. Well, perhaps not so patiently: I was having a total anxiety attack as the reality of what we were doing started to set in. My partner was due to be inseminated only six hours prior to my own embryo transfer. What if both procedures were successful? The doctor had told Kristen that he saw *four* viable eggs during the examination he'd given her the day before. She could end up with quadruplets *herself*!

I stole a glance at Kristen. She was thumbing through an issue of *Rolling Stone* with a half smile on her face. I knew she believed we'd both get pregnant that day, that fourteen months of negative and heartbreaking results had led us right to that moment. It was fate, she'd said earlier, that had brought us to the doctor's office on the exact same day once again. "Kristen H.?" the nurse called, and I tried to banish the fearful thoughts from my mind. They certainly weren't helping me prepare for *my* procedure.

After Kristen's IUI insemination, we went downstairs to a luncheonette for coffee and pancakes. Knowing that Kristen was now potentially pregnant, I could not stop my mind from tumbling down the rabbit hole. "What if you're pregnant with twins?" I uttered in a voice laced with fear. "And what if they transfer two embryos into me this afternoon and we're *both* pregnant with twins by the end of the day?"

"That could happen!" she exclaimed. "I hope it does!" By the look on her face, I could tell she was serious.

"Stop talking like that; you are *completely* stressing me out!" I said.

"Sorry—the last thing I want to do right now is stress you out before your procedure." She paused. "Let's stop talking so I can fantasize about our two sets of twins. What will we name them all? Okay, I'm done—I'll stop talking!"

I fixed her with a final glare and said, "Thank you. Please. Stop talking."

As we headed back to the doctor's office for the embryo transfer, I felt a flutter in my throat. It had been such a long road. Now here I was, sitting in my all-too-familiar clinic, awaiting the fate of my embryos. Would they be viable enough to transfer? And once transferred, would any survive to become a full-blown pregnancy? Then, of course, I had to make it through the first trimester. I rubbed my hands together and realized they were sweating. "Is this going to work?" I whispered to Kristen.

"Absolutely. This is absolutely going to work," she responded. Moments later, I was sitting on the examination table in my white gown, waiting for the doctor to arrive. Kristen sat in a nearby chair. As the doctor entered the room, he glanced at Kristen, then gave me a quizzical look. He was the same doctor who'd inseminated her that morning—our usual doctor was away for the holiday weekend.

He turned back to me and said, "You've got two good embryos here. We're going to transfer both of them today. Are you ready?"

"What are my chances of becoming pregnant with these two embryos?" I asked, my voice quivering.

"Your chances are extremely good," he replied. "I'd put them at fifty percent."

I'd always been able to squeeze a silver lining out of the darkest of situations, but trying and failing to get pregnant so many times had left me less optimistic. I was having a hard time believing this could ever work. I thought maybe I was not supposed to have children and this was God's way of telling me I'd be a terrible mom. I had already decided that if this IVF procedure did not work, I would not do it again. It seemed like the doctor could sense my worry, because he said, "Both embryos we are transferring today are healthy and strong. You are in great shape here." Then he glanced back at Kristen, again with a confused look on his face.

I finally blurted, "We're trying to increase our chances."

Kristen's face reddened and she said, "Hi, yes, we met earlier this morning. Thanks for all your help today." With that, they wheeled me off for the big transfer.

I dozed off in the recovery room, only to be woken up a half hour later by a nurse hovering over me. From far away I heard her ask, "Would you like your husband to join you while you lie in recovery?"

"That would be fantastic, but I don't do husbands," I said as I woke up. "My partner, Kristen, is in the waiting room."

She was a younger nurse with a hip blunt haircut; she laughed and said, "Oh, cool! I'll go get her."

Kristen entered my cubicle recovery area in the middle of a full-blown conversation with the nurse about her band. "Actually, we're playing a festival in July," she was saying.

"I'm on your e-mail list!" the nurse exclaimed. "Will you send an announcement about that date?"

"Definitely," Kristen replied. "Honey, can you believe your nurse is a fan of the band?"

I was about to respond when the doctor entered the room. "The transfer of both embryos went extremely well today, Sarah," he said. "And, Kristen, you had four viable follicles inseminated this morning. I would say the odds of someone in your family being pregnant are very hopeful."

My nurse/Kristen's fan interjected, "*Whoa*—you're *both* trying?"

I always thought it was cool when Kristen got recognized by people, but this was not exactly a moment I wanted to share with a fan.

I did not need to read about our dual pregnancy attempt on "Page Six" in the *New York Post,* at least not at this stage of our process. But there we all were, caught in an incredibly awkward moment.

"We are, actually, but, you know . . . we're keeping it private," Kristen said in an attempt to defuse the situation.

"Of course, of course, I totally understand," the nurse told us. "Good luck—this is *so* exciting!" She turned to me. "Now, just lay still. I'll be back to help you get up in a bit." The nurse left us half-confident our secret was safe with her.

The doctor continued. "So, Sarah, we'll see you back in the office later this week for a blood test. Take it easy for the next few days and call us if you have any concerns." He turned and left the room.

"Your fan was my nurse for the embryo transfer," I told Kristen. "Bizarre," I giggled, and dozed off.

An hour later, we were back on the streets of New York City hailing a cab. The waiting game had officially begun. The week passed slowly, and every cramp was suspect. Our conversations were reduced to the following:

"I feel something. Do you think it's gas?"

"Oh God. I think I'm spotting. Does this look pink to you?"

"I am totally premenstrual; I'm getting my period any second."

Kristen was especially guilty of feeling premenstrual. Within a day of her insemination she was convinced she was getting her period, which didn't give me much time to worry about how my own procedure had gone. A week after my transfer, I went into the fertility clinic for a pregnancy test. Two hours later I got a call from a very stoic nurse, saying, "Hi, Sarah, congratulations—your results are positive. We'll see you on Friday for a head count."

"What's a head count?" I asked eagerly.

"A head count means they're checking to see how many embryos successfully implanted," the nurse answered.

I hung up the phone and called Kristen, who was on her way to an afternoon therapy session. "I'm pregnant!" I said.

"Ha, thank God!" said Kristen. "Now I don't feel upset that I'm *not* pregnant."

"We don't know that you're *not* pregnant, Kristen! You need to take a test."

"I'm not spending another dime on those pregnancy tests; anyway I have to wait a week. It would never show up now, it's too early. You're *pregnant*—we're having a baby! Who cares what I am!" Kristen crowed, forgetting all about our pledge to keep a lid on our happiness. Of course, I couldn't blame her for not wanting to spend more money on a pregnancy test. We had just received amazing news. The last thing either of us needed was to read another negative result. Kristen carried on celebrating my pregnancy as if there wasn't even the slightest possibility that she might be pregnant, too.

A few days later, I couldn't wait anymore: *"Please* go downstairs and buy a pregnancy test so we can end my agony—I *have* to know if we're both pregnant!" I cried.

Kristin protested. "It's a waste of money, I'm telling you. I am getting my period by morning; I can feel it. But okay, if you insist, I'll pick up a pregnancy test along with a box of tampons." Fifteen minutes later, she returned with the goods and entered the bathroom. I stood in front of the door while she peed on the stick. She finished and handed the test over without giving it so much as a glance.

"Baby, you're pregnant—we're *both* pregnant!" I shouted in utter disbelief. Then I stared at her, astonished.

Kristen grabbed the stick out of my hands and looked at it. "My God, you're right!" she said. "This is *awesome!*" And she sank back down to the toilet, staring at the test.

My mind jumped from thought to thought with alarming alacrity: How could this have happened? The goal had been *one* baby, not two. Who was going to take care of *me?* The next nine months were supposed to be *The Sarah Show,* costarring her supportive and loving partner, Kristen. Who was going to fill my every craving at the oddest hours of the night? Who was going to rub my feet? How could I complain hourly of aches and pains and invent phantom ones? There went my nine months of not lifting a finger to take out the garbage, move the car, or traipse upstairs for a forgotten item. I hadn't even been given a full week to bask in the glory of my new "with child" status. It was obvious from the phone conversation Kristen had with her mother while still sitting on the toilet seat that she was not having the same thoughts.

"Mom, we're *both* pregnant!" she cried. "Can you imagine anything more fun than this?" And to think *I'd* pushed Kristen to get that pregnancy test.

Chapter 8

Talk of the Town

Kristen

When a second neon line came beaming off the stick, I was stunned. Staring at it, I felt as if I had never read a pregnancy test before.

"Is that plus sign in the window there before you pee?" I asked.

"No!" Sarah said insistently. "Plus signs only show up if you're pregnant!"

"But there's only one plus sign," I said, trying to prove I could not possibly be pregnant. "Maybe the window on the other end of the stick is supposed to match?"

"Kristen," Sarah said, pacing back and forth in front of the bathroom door. "Pregnancy-stick makers would not let a plus sign turn up on a negative pregnancy test. It would cause pandemonium in the streets. A plus sign on a pregnancy stick means you are pregnant!"

"Hand me the phone, I have to call my mom!" I exclaimed as I fell back down onto the toilet seat in happy shock. Sarah and I had agreed that if we got pregnant this time around, we would not tell our friends or families until we were out of the first trimester. But we did make one exception: our nosy mothers.

For the past six months, my fertility treatment had turned me into a raging bull, and my mother had been my primary target. I could barely speak to her without picking a fight. I felt the least I could do was let her know this period of abuse had finally paid off: Fingers crossed, I would be delivering a grandchild to her within nine months.

"I have some news," I began when my mother picked up the phone.

"You're pregnant!" she screamed. "Honey, she's pregnant! Uncork the champagne! Oh, this is so exciting!"

I interrupted. "Mom, we're *both* pregnant! Can you imagine anything more fun than this?"

"What?" the pitch of my mother's voice shifted two octaves higher.

I laughed and blurted out, "Sarah's pregnant too!"

There was a long pause on the other end of the line as my mother took in this remarkable piece of information; she'd had no idea Sarah had been trying again.

"Mom? Are you there?" I asked, thinking the line had been disconnected.

"Did you say Sarah's pregnant too?" she finally asked, astonished. As I heard the phone hit the ground, my mother screamed with excitement, "Frank! They're *both* pregnant!"

Sarah

During the first month of our pregnancies, we flip-flopped between caution and excitement. We didn't want to get ahead of ourselves like last time but couldn't contain our elation. We were also both in total shock. We spent hours repeating the news to each other. "We're both really pregnant?" we said to one another on a nightly basis. I started peeing on pregnancy sticks just to feel the joy of getting positive results. After spending so many months getting negative ones, I loved seeing a positive line pop up on the sticks. It became an expensive—but very satisfying—thrill. At work, I sat at my desk with a half smile on my face, no doubt confusing my coworkers, who were probably wondering where Medusa had gone.

Though Kristen would never admit it, she had been half-asleep since the day after her insemination—a surefire sign she was pregnant. I, on the other hand, was able to ward off any symptoms for the first few weeks. Of course, this worried me to no end. I confided in my doctor at my first sonogram appointment. "I'm not having any pregnancy symptoms at all. They say symptoms are a sign of a healthy pregnancy. Do you think I'm still pregnant?"

He started laughing out loud. "You're definitely pregnant, no doubt about it. From what I can see, both embryos have implanted in the wall of your uterus."

"Sorry—did you just say *both* embryos?" I asked.

"That's right; as of now, you're having twins."

"We're having *three babies!*" Kristen screamed with excitement.

"That's impossible; please tell me you're kidding!" I blurted out. I started doing the math in my head. How would we pay for three college educations at the same time? We didn't have enough bedrooms in the house we'd just bought. And we still had two years of payments left on a car that wouldn't fit three car seats. "How likely is it that I will carry these two babies to term?" I asked, trying not to reveal my near-total hysteria.

"To be honest, it's not very likely you will carry both embryos to term," the doctor said with kindness in his voice, as if he thought I was pleased with the news that I was having twins. "It's so early in your pregnancy; most women haven't realized they've missed their period at this point. We'll keep an eye on them every week and see how the embryos progress."

I was relieved I had fooled him; I didn't need our doctor to think he'd just impregnated an ice queen with no maternal drive. As soon as we left his office, I prepared to call my mother. She already knew I was pregnant, but I had yet to tell her Kristen was, too. Now I didn't know which news to divulge first.

"Should I tell her I'm pregnant with twins?" I asked Kristen as we waited to cross the street. "Or do I tell her that you're pregnant, too?"

"Yes," Kristen responded.

"What do you mean, yes?" I smacked Kristen's arm.

"I mean tell her everything!" she said. "Tell her you're pregnant with twins and I'm pregnant as well. *And* tell her we'll be going back to the doctor at the end of the week to see if I'm carrying multiples!" When the light changed, she practically skipped across the street.

"How can this possibly be happening to us?" I moaned.

"I'm not listening to you right now," Kristen sang, covering her ears with her hands. "We're getting a minivan!"

"We are *not* getting a minivan!" I hissed. "We'll discuss this later. I have to call my mother."

After my last pregnancy, my mother had sent out a press release to all of Staten Island. She'd had a lot of backtracking to do when I'd miscarried. So this time, when I told her I was pregnant she barely reacted. I am sure part of her would have preferred not to find out until after the first trimester. Little did she know, I was about to hit her with an even bigger shock.

To her, the news that I was carrying twins was nothing compared to finding out Kristen was pregnant, too. We never told her Kristen had started trying to conceive, so the announcement rendered her speechless. It took twenty minutes of explaining to my father before he finally understood we were *both* pregnant. He never quite grasped that I was carrying two babies. By the time we found out I had a "disappearing twin," as the doctor put it, we no longer had to worry about it.

I thought I would be relieved to get the news that one of my two embryos had reabsorbed into my body. I no longer had to worry about three mouths to feed, we could stop looking at minivans, and we did not have to sell our brand-new house. Yet there I was, frozen on the same couch I'd lived on during my miscarriage. "I lost another baby," I cried to Kristen, who tried her best to comfort me, though she seemed even sadder than I was. She'd been looking forward to having three babies the whole time.

"It just wasn't meant to be, honey, that's all," she said. "We have to stay positive for the two little babies inside of us." I knew she was right, but now that I was carrying only one baby, I felt that old terror creeping in again. For the seven weeks I had two babies inside of me, I'd felt like I had some insurance. That night, I went to sleep as devastated as I'd been after my first miscarriage. I knew I had to pull myself together for the baby I was carrying, but I just needed one night to mourn my loss.

Kristen

The morning after we found out that one of Sarah's twins had "disappeared," I started spotting. I insisted that Sarah come into the bathroom to gauge whether she thought I was making a big deal out of nothing.

"I don't think you're overreacting," she said with a worried look on her face. I called the fertility doctor and left a message. An hour later, a nurse returned my phone call.

"Kristen, it's totally normal to spot," she said, attempting to comfort me. "Seventy percent of pregnant women spot during their first trimester. But you should put a call in to your ob-gyn to be sure everything is okay."

Unfortunately, I did not have my own ob-gyn to call. In all the fuss of trying to get pregnant, I overlooked the task of calling Sarah's ob-gyn to make an appointment for myself. Over the course of the next few hours, my spotting got heavier. Panic set in: We were about to lose two babies in two days! Sarah called her ob-gyn and told them our story.

"We really shouldn't take on any new patients at this time," the receptionist said, "but your situation is so unique. Come in right away. The doctor will do a sonogram to make sure everything is all right."

"She'll see me right away?" I cried. I just needed to be told that my baby's heart was beating.

Sarah and I raced to the office and didn't even bother to fill out the new-patient paperwork; we just sprinted into the ultrasound room. By then, the spotting had turned to bleeding. Five months earlier, when Sarah had been lying on this table, Sheila the sonographer had told us she no longer detected a heartbeat. We'd both cried as she'd comforted two virtual strangers through the worst news they'd ever received. Now I was convinced that what had happened to Sarah was happening to me. I pictured how crushed I would be, trying to put on a brave face while Sarah carried our only remaining baby to full term. I climbed onto the sonogram table, grabbed Sarah's hand, and closed my eyes. In my mind, I had already lost the baby.

"There it is," Sheila said, pointing to a line moving on the screen. "The baby's heartbeat is there. See it? It's totally fine."

"The heartbeat is strong?" I repeated. "The baby is okay?"

"It's totally normal to spot," she said, trying to reassure us. "I know it's worrisome after all you two have been through, but your baby's heartbeat is strong. Everything is fine this time." She left the room.

I spent the next few days in a constant state of worry. Any chance I got I would check for spotting. And every time, there was nothing there. Still, each night, as soon as Sarah got home from work, I'd summon her to the bathroom for a second opinion.

"Are you sure you don't see a pink spot?" I'd say, holding the toilet paper up to the light.

"Kristen, you're not spotting anymore," Sarah said insistently. "Please stop going to the bathroom."

But I was unable to keep it together. Any morning I woke up without morning sickness, I was convinced I was on the verge of a miscarriage. My days were filled with bathroom checks and Google searches trying to pair up my symptoms with "worst-case scenario" pregnancy stories.

This also happened to be the week that Antigone Rising played the Great South Bay Music Festival on Long Island. My doctor had given me the okay to perform, but I was nervous about the amount of stress I was going to be under. It was a blazing hot day in July, the first show we were going to do as a foursome, and Cathy and I were singing lead vocals. I had no idea how the crowd would react, or if we'd even be able to draw a crowd. In the end, everything went as smoothly as we could have hoped. Despite the swampy weather, the crowd was huge and the reaction was very positive.

But a few days later, I started spotting again. This time it was bright red and heavy from the onset. I called the doctor's office. Once again, a nurse assured me that as long as I was not cramping, I had nothing to worry about.

"That's not what the Internet search says—according to all these women, they started spotting without cramps, just like I've been," I said, my voice trembling with fear.

"You should stay away from the Internet at a time like this," the nurse said. Later that day, the spotting had me so worked up I was convinced I felt cramps. At that point, the ob-gyn allowed me to come in for a second sonogram.

A year and a half earlier, I had gone into the whole "let's make a baby" process very nonchalantly. I figured we would both get pregnant when it was the right time. I knew it was a process over which I had no control. And back then, I was totally at peace with that notion. But after Sarah's miscarriage and nine months of Clomid between the two of us, I was a complete wreck, convinced each day of my first trimester was the day I was going to lose the baby. In my mind I had already miscarried once before, even though I knew logically I had not physically miscarried. While it made perfect sense to me, it was absolute nonsense to the many doctors and nurses I harassed during those first eleven weeks.

"You didn't suffer a miscarriage, Kristen," Sheila said as I lay on the table for my second sonogram in as many weeks. "You have no history of losing pregnancies. You are not Sarah. This baby you are carrying is fine. See the heart beating?" She pointed to the monitor. Even Sarah stopped meeting me at the doctor's office. I was on my own, spotting daily with a perfectly healthy baby growing inside me. It was enough to drive a pregnant woman mad. Eventually the spotting would stop, but it would start up again a few days later. So, during my first trimester, it became something I was forced to live with. It did, however, prevent me from telling anyone I was pregnant until I knew for sure that I was safe.

At the tail end of our first trimesters, we went on vacation to Provincetown, Massachusetts, with several good friends. It was Family Week in Ptown, a week dedicated to celebrating families of all orientations, and we rented a house on the water with Sally, Gigi, and the dogs, Tucker and Willi (Sally's black lab). Unfortunately, it was not going to be the "pregnancy coming-out party" Sarah had hoped for.

"I'm not telling anyone I am pregnant," I told Sarah. "You can tell whomever you want that you are. Just don't drag me into the story."

"How do you suppose I do that, Kristen? I can't tell all our friends I'm pregnant while my closeted pregnant partner looks on."

"Of course you can," I said as we entered the local coffee shop on the west end of town. "We'll have two decafs," I said to the man behind the counter.

"Decaf? What's the point?" chortled a heavyset gay man standing in line behind me. Clearly, he'd been out late the night before, with his red-rimmed eyes and two-day stubble.

I turned to him and said, "We're pregnant. We're both pregnant. We can't drink caffeine. None of our friends knows we're pregnant, though. It's too early to tell people. So if you see us in town this week, you can't say anything to our friends!"

"Are you serious?" he screamed. "That is *so* exciting—I love secrets! You girls are crazy. You're both pregnant? Together? How did you ever work that out? I'm going to be repeating this story all week! I just hope we don't run into each other when I've had a few drinks." He poured some sweetener into his coffee, began stirring, and waited to hear the rest of the story.

"We used the same donor and both conceived on the same day, relatively speaking," I said. Technically, Sarah's embryo was three days ahead of mine due to her IVF procedure, but I didn't think I needed to get into that with the stocky gay man in the coffee shop on Cape Cod.

"Good luck to you both and God bless!" he said as he walked out of the shop.

I could feel Sarah's eyes boring into me as though I'd lost my mind. "What?" I said. "At least if I miscarry, I won't feel obligated to track him down and tell him what happened." Informing a total stranger seemed perfectly logical to me; I just wanted to be sure I was in the clear before making any announcements to family and friends.

"Are you sure you're not still on the Clomid?" Sarah asked as she shook her head, picked up her coffee, and walked out into the sunshine.

Sarah

Toward the end of our annual Cape Cod vacation, two of our good friends, Rikki and Christina—who happened to be lawyers—began to cross-examine us. They found it suspicious that we would leave the beach to get ice cream during the day, only to be discovered later that night eating more ice cream. The first time it happened, we all laughed about it on the street. "You know how it is on vacation,"

I said. "Screw all diets!" The second time we ran into Rikki and Christina while holding towering cones of ice cream, we all laughed again, though they didn't let us get off as easy.

"Okay, seriously, what is it with you guys?" Rikki asked, eyeing my three scoops of mint chocolate chip on a giant waffle cone. "Ever heard of bikini season?"

"It's fat-free yogurt," I lied as Kristen shot me a knowing look.

The following morning, Kristen and I planted ourselves on the beach. Rikki and Christina met up with us soon after. I attempted to turn my chair away from the group as I slid a dill pickle out of my lunch bag. From the moment the deli man had included it with my sandwich I hadn't been able to get it off my mind. The craving was so strong I had no choice but to eat it as soon as we found our patch of sand for the day. As I crunched down on the dill, Rikki jumped to her feet, ready to confront my bizarre behavior. "Sarah!" she said sharply as all eyes turned to me. "What are you eating?"

I stopped midcrunch and looked up at her with big, guilty eyes. Having failed to prepare a backup story, I said sheepishly, "A pickle? I bought it for lunch, but I'm hungry now."

That's when Christina went in for the kill. "Okay, the jig is up: What do you guys want to tell us? Ice cream twice a day, now pickles for breakfast? Spill it, you two."

I locked eyes with Kristen. That morning marked my thirteenth week of pregnancy. Technically, I was in the clear to make the announcement. Kristen, who was still two days away from her second trimester, was extremely superstitious. The night before, while we were sitting on the porch of our rental house, Sally had begun prodding as to why we weren't drinking. Uncomfortable lying, Kristen and I broke our rule and told her and Gigi our news, swearing they'd be the only ones to find out until Kristen was officially in the clear. Gigi was elated for us, and we let her stay up past her bedtime picking out names and imagining what the genders might be. Now, only twelve hours later and with all eyes on us, we knew we were going to have to tell our friends something. "Should we?" I asked Kristen. She nodded yes. This was our first time telling anyone outside our family. No matter how I put it, they were going to be shocked. I figured I'd just go for it.

"Guess who's pregnant?" I asked. I knew this approach would take them off guard and buy me a minute to think my story through.

"What do you mean guess who's pregnant?" Christina asked. "*You* are!" She and I had spent the prior afternoon at the hotel swimming pool, where she'd seen me in my bikini; I was definitely starting to show.

"You are correct," I said, "but someone else is, too!" Christina's face became contorted with confusion.

"What do you mean?" she asked. "Who else is pregnant?" Then she spun around and looked at Kristen. "Wait—*you're pregnant, too?*"

Kristen smiled. "Indeed I am," she said.

"*What?!*" Christina and Rikki erupted in unison. After several congratulatory hugs, questions flew at us from all angles: Was this planned? How were we going to manage dual pregnancies? When were we both due? Fortunately, we had answers to the first few, but then the inquiries started getting tougher and tougher: How were we going to give birth and manage the first few months? What if we went into labor on the same day? What if one going into labor set the other one off? Who was going to be in the delivery room? We were getting a baby nurse, right?

Just coming out of the nauseous haze of our first trimester, clearly we hadn't thought through all the details. However, we had decided on a few things: "Lizzy will be called into active duty," I said. "I'm sure she'll be practically living with us while helping us out. Our mothers might be in the delivery room; we're still debating that one. And hopefully we'll have a baby nurse—we *are* New Yorkers."

This was only our *first* round of tough questioning! It wasn't any easier for me at work once I finally shared the news about our dual pregnancies. A few weeks after our trip to the cape, the managing editor of the magazine stopped a meeting midway through, wanting answers to some questions. "How are you and Kristen going to handle the hormone haze that immediately follows giving birth?" she demanded as my entire marketing department stared at me. "After I gave birth, I didn't know which end was up. Emotionally and physically, I was a mess!"

"We are seriously going to have to wing it, because it's going to be a shit show starring Sarah and Kristen and our two little new babies," I said as the room cracked up. "*Or* I can buy our way through this pickle and we'll get help at every turn: night nurses, day nurses, doulas, housekeepers. I am open to any and all suggestions."

"Well, you are going to need your mothers," the managing editor said.

"Oh, no worries there, we've got them in bulk," I joked. "It's managing *them* that will be the bigger problem."

The more friends and extended family members Kristen and I told, the more pleasure we derived out of shocking them. "Guess which one of us is pregnant!" became our favorite game. Essentially, we were forcing people to tell us who looked fatter. Some were smart enough not to play along. Others got the joke right away and realized both of us were knocked up. Most people guessed that I was the pregnant one. I could have taken offense; instead, I convinced myself they knew I'd been trying. In the end, Kristen gained a lot more pregnancy weight than I did. So I can look back on the game and laugh about being the technical loser.

As our bellies grew, so did the curiosity of people we'd see in our everyday lives. Our building's doorman, pharmacy clerks, and the waitress at our favorite diner all bombarded us with questions when we told them our news. "Once the babies are born, people won't ask so many questions," I told Kristen with confidence. I couldn't know it at the time, but the sight of us with two babies would evoke almost as many questions as the sight of our two pregnant bellies. Ours would be a story we'd be telling for years.

Six-year-old Sarah and 7-year-old Spencer in backyard
on Staten Island. *Photo by Ken Ellis*

Kristen (5 years old) and brother Tommy
(1 year old) on front lawn in Glen Cove, N.Y.
Photo by Frank Henderson

Kristen onstage in Palm Springs, California, 2007. *Photo by Cindy Lea Hall*

Antigone Rising live onstage at Brooklyn Bowl, Williamsburg, Brooklyn. l. to r. Cathy Henderson, Nini Camps, Dena Tauriello, Kristen Henderson. *Photo by Warren Chow*

Kristen and Lizzy playing *Grand Theft Auto* at 20th Street apartment, 2007. *Photo by Sarah Ellis*

Kristen and Sarah meet,
Boston, New Year's Eve 2005.
Photo by Jen Bonner

Sarah and Kristen, April 17, 2007, after getting their
domestic partnership. Celebration lunch at Cafe Cluny
(West Village, NYC). *Photo by the waiter*

Kristen and Sarah with their mothers at the Long Island
baby shower, January 10, 2009. *Photo by Frank Henderson*

Kristen and Sarah at the Staten Island baby shower,
December 2008. *Photo by Paul Pawlowski*

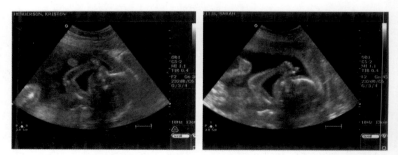

First photos of Thomas and Kate—identical positions! *Cityscape OBGyn*

Strategizing with doula Jen in the delivery room at NYU Medical Center before Thomas was born, February 1, 2009. *Photo by Katie Ambrose*

Pop Pop and Peapa holding Thomas in the hospital. *Photo taken by Kristen Henderson, from her hospital bed*

Thomas and Kate bond on Sarah's belly. Tucker gets in on the action, too. Waiting for Kate to arrive, early February 2009. *Photo by Kristen Henderson*

Katie's here! February 24, 2009. *Photo by doula Jen Dembo*

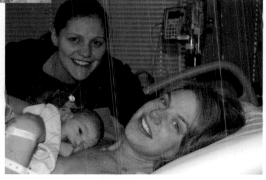

Kate and Thomas spend their first night together, February 26, 2009.
Photo by Kristen Henderson

The Ellis and Henderson families celebrate the christening of the twins,
St. John's Episcopal Church, Staten Island, N.Y., June 7, 2009.
Photo by Tip Henderson

Thomas eats chocolate cake, 1st birthday, February 2010. *Photo by Kristen Henderson*

Katie eats chocolate cake, 1st birthday, February 2010. *Photo by Kristen Henderson*

Mike and Janet Perrotta with the twins. *Photo by Kristen Henderson*

Sarah with the twins in kitchen. *Photo by Lizzy Brooks*

Thomas as Santa and Kate as Frosty, first Halloween.
Photo by Kristen Henderson

At home with Tucker. *Photo by Katie Ambrose*

Chapter 9

She Said, She Said

Kristen

By our second trimester, our monthly weigh-ins had become increasingly competitive. And I was winning—that is, if gaining more weight every month was a good thing. I'd already found out I wasn't carrying multiples. But I might as well have been, considering the fact that I'd gained ten pounds at each weigh-in for several months in a row. One month, we had to come in a week earlier than usual. Because I'd just been weighed three weeks earlier, I stepped onto the scale sure my weight gain would be in the single digits.

"Wow, this was a big month for you!" the nurse said, staring at my chart in disbelief.

"How big of a month?" I asked nervously.

"Oh my," she said. "Your last visit was only three weeks ago?"

"Yes, it was. Which is why I'm sure whatever you're about to tell me is wrong. You need to reweigh me."

"Sorry, the scale doesn't lie. You gained sixteen pounds in three weeks. What have you been *eating*?" the nurse laughed.

"Anything that isn't nailed down," I replied. I was mortified.

By the middle of my second trimester, I had already gained

forty pounds, with no signs of slowing down. I had started off so well, eating vegetables and fruits. Back then, I'd stuck to the rule that I needed no more than an additional three hundred calories per day during pregnancy. But somewhere along the way, I'd lost my resolve—and I knew exactly who was responsible. Aside from my own strange pregnancy cravings, I'd begun partaking in Sarah's. Unfortunately, hers came in cartons found in the freezer aisle, usually topped with whipped cream and cherries. Of course, I did step aside and watch in awe when it came to her more eccentric cravings. We would often visit our favorite diner, and as soon as the waitress stopped by our table, I knew what was coming.

"Do you have Wonder Bread?" Sarah would ask.

"We have white bread," the waitress would reply.

"I'd really prefer Wonder Bread; it's thicker than white bread," Sarah would say insistently.

"I can check for you, ma'am."

"Okay, assuming you have it, I'd like a tomato sandwich on Wonder Bread with salt and mayonnaise. Oh—and a pickle and chocolate shake. Please."

After staring at her for a long moment, the waitress would say, "Okay . . . I'll check." Then she would scurry away from the table, glancing over her shoulder as if she'd just realized she was waiting on a woman who was giving birth to a sixties-era space alien.

Once Sarah got her highly specific—and, frankly, disgusting— order fulfilled, she would bite down on the pickle and chase it with a gulp of chocolate shake. The thought made me gag.

"It must be a pregnant thing," Sarah would say insistently.

"But I'm pregnant too!" I'd reply.

"Well, we obviously have different cravings," she would sniff, and leave it at that.

In the beginning, my cravings were very specific but also extremely healthy. I would call every diner in New York City until I found one whose soup of the day was lentil bean. Split pea would not suffice. It had to be lentil, accompanied by a grilled Swiss cheese sandwich on whole wheat bread. I ate that meal every night for one month straight. All day long I'd snack on apples. After munching into a chilled Red Delicious, I would follow it with a spoonful of grated Romano cheese, the type you sprinkle over pasta.

Eventually, the cravings got less and less healthy. For lunch, I'd eat two peanut butter and jelly sandwiches and wash them down with a big glass of milk. The sandwiches had to be made with gobs and gobs of peanut butter, enough to gag a normal person. Before long, the cravings turned to vanilla ice cream with bananas, topped with whipped cream. I'd call Big Daddy's Diner in the wee hours of the night and beg them to send over an ice cream sundae, even though I was well below the minimum delivery charge. If the deliveryman arrived with a dish full of melted-vanilla-ice-cream-and-banana soup, even better. I'd drink it from the foil container (though I could never understand the chocolate-milkshake-and-pickles craving). Inevitably, my binges were followed by the worst case of hiccups I'd ever felt. The reason I say "felt" instead of "heard" is because I was not the one doing the hiccupping. It appeared that my carbon-ated-beverage craving was causing an issue for the tenant inside my womb, who was going to hiccup their way out of my stomach. Some nights, I could actually see my stomach pulsating.

In my opinion, I gained an ungodly amount of weight during that second trimester, but the nurse always assured me I was okay. "Just slow down on the sweets and make sure you're continuing to eat leafy greens," she said. I promised I'd try, but *she* wasn't the one carrying a sugar-crazed offensive tackle with what seemed like a pending penchant for banana-flavored breast milk. The next time I sat down for lunch, I looked at my bulging belly and tried to resist its demands. I failed miserably.

Sarah

The second trimester was marked by Kristen's extreme, and at times irrational, laughter. *Everything* made her laugh. And it wasn't a typical Kristen laugh. It was a deep-down guttural laugh, the type reserved for a jolly, heavyset person, which was exactly what my partner had become. Not to mention that no one was exempt from being laughed at. News of our friend's untimely job loss was funny to Kristen. She knew it was inappropriate but had no control over the hysterical laughing fit that followed our friend's tearful voice mail message. "She just bought a new place—that's got to be so stressful," Kristen said, choking, with her hand over her mouth. "She never should have bought that cramped shithole of an apartment!" Then she doubled over, slapping her knee.

When her band was in the studio one day, recording, she laughed her way through an entire vocal pass. The producer interrupted on the talk-back mic and said, "Kristen, you do realize we're paying by the hour in this place?"

Tears streamed down Kristen's face. "I know; sorry, maybe Cathy can sing my part? These lyrics are just so stupid!" She cracked up.

"You wrote them, Kristen," the producer said. Upon hearing this, she laughed even harder.

Once, a total stranger tripped and fell in front of us on the sidewalk, which caused Kristen to double over at the knees, heaving and slapping her leg as people rushed to help him up. One weekend, we rented the movie *Baby Mama* with Tina Fey and Amy Poehler. During one scene, Amy's character sticks gum under Tina's character's coffee table and then denies that she did it. When Kristen saw this, she laughed so hard she actually wet her pants. "I think I might need an oxygen mask," she gasped as she excused herself to go to the bathroom. Days and weeks later, she would burst out laughing over that same scene. Jokes that Kristen would have deemed downright unfunny in a prior life now caused her to dissolve into hysterics. Her entire second trimester was spent in a hormonal, hysterical guffaw, so when it came time for us to start discussing extremely serious matters, such as testing for birth abnormalities or finding out our babies' genders, Kristen's inability to hold a serious conversation really worked against us.

During our sixteen-week appointment, our ob-gyn, Dr. Rosenbaum, asked, "So, ladies, have you discussed whether or not you will be having amniocentesis exams? You're coming up on the window during which the test can still be performed." Several weeks earlier, she'd said we needed to decide whether or not to perform that risky and invasive procedure so that she could rule out several genetic abnormalities. "What do you think?" she said, pressing us.

Kristen and I answered simultaneously:

"Yes."

"No."

"You've decided to have it? Or not?" she asked, puzzled. For some reason, that question set Kristen off; she started to laugh uncontrollably. Dr. Rosenbaum just stared at her. She was a fairly serious woman, dressed in gray slacks and a sensible white button-down shirt, with a pair of bifocals hanging from a chain around her neck. "This is usually a decision the expectant couple is in agreement on," she said, knitting her brows together and making a note in our charts.

"We *are* in agreement," Kristen choked out between peals of laughter. "Sarah is having one and I am not!"

"I want to advise you both since you're each over thirty-five years of age, there are increased risks for serious genetic abnormalities that could put both you and the babies at risk should you decide to carry full-term," she said, completely ignoring the fact that Kristen was now doubled over, gasping for air. "I don't foresee either of your pregnancies being at risk, and there are several less invasive exams we can perform before the amniocentesis that will indicate whether or not we should proceed with the riskier one. How does that sound?"

Again, we simultaneously responded:

"I'm having one."

"I'm not having one."

"Okay, you two," Dr. Rosenbaum said, growing stern. "This really is something you may want to get on the same page about. Let's discuss it after you've had a chance to talk it over at home." Kristen and I agreed we would talk about it, each of us secretly thinking we would convince the other to do what we wanted by the time of our next visit. "And at that time," Dr. Rosenbaum said, "we will be able to detect the babies' genders."

"I definitely want to find out the baby's gender," I replied without hesitation.

"I have no intention of finding out the baby's gender," Kristen said. "And Sarah's not finding out the gender, either."

"Yes I am! And so are you! One baby will have a room full of gender-appropriate gifts and the other will have a shower filled with green and yellow bibs and blankets? That's not happening to one of my babies!"

Dr. Rosenbaum looked from one of us to the other; clearly, she was not going to lack for dinner table conversation that night. "So, one of you will be finding out the gender and the other will not?" she said. "Is that correct? May I ask what you two talk about in your spare time?"

"We talk about how Kristen wants to deliver in a pool outside in the yard and I want to be hooked up to an epidural a week prior to going into labor," I said, and started to laugh, causing Kristen to dissolve into a new round of hysteria. She had to wipe tears off her face, she was laughing so hard.

"We are planning to have a doula with us in the delivery room," Kristen said, though she could barely get the words out between laughs.

"A *doula*?" I cried.

"You most certainly can have a doula in your delivery room as long as you're both in agreement about it," Dr. Rosenbaum said, finally starting to laugh herself. "It's really time for you two to hammer out some details. Maybe by the next visit you will be a little more in sync?"

A month later, I was leaving work to meet Kristen and both of our mothers at A Pea in the Pod to shop for maternity clothes. Immediately following, we were all going to head over to Dr. Rosenbaum's office for our highly anticipated baby gender sonograms. Kristen and I had both decided to skip the amniocentesis exams. Twenty of my coworkers cheered as I strolled toward the elevator on my way to the appointment, each of them shouting out their final guesses. I was buzzing with excitement; by the time I returned to the office, I would know if I was going to give birth to a boy or a girl—I couldn't wait! Kristen, on the other hand, planned to remain in the dark until she gave birth. This forced us into planning a neutral nursery, as well as selecting the most boring baby items imaginable for our registry. The whole idea of waiting to find out the gender was completely lost on me. Wouldn't there be enough surprises between now and February? The added suspense felt unnecessary, and, frankly, selfish on her part. I was downright angry with Kristen for forcing one of our unborn babies to be stuck with gender-neutral baby swag. So much so that I barely spoke to her as we entered the doctor's office.

Kristen

From the second our mothers knew we were pregnant, they had been planning on joining us for the big "gender reveal" appointment. In their minds, this was the event of the century. By the time Sarah got changed, I was already on the table in my gown, flanked by both of our mothers. If Sarah was going to ruin the surprise of finding out what she was carrying, I wanted to make her wait as long as humanly possible to find out. Once again, Sheila the sonographer slathered my belly with gel and waved her little wand back and forth.

"You don't want to know the gender, right?" she asked.

Sarah piped up from across the room. "Can you believe her, Sheila?"

"Listen, some people don't like to know," Sheila said. "I prefer knowing myself. It makes planning for the nursery and things so much easier. But I can understand a first-time mother wanting to be surprised." She turned back to the screen. "This baby's got ten fingers and ten toes. Everything looks really good here, Kristen. And I can tell what it is, just so you know."

"What is it?" I blurted, shocking myself with the question. How could Sheila the sonographer know what I was having while I did not?

"Are you sure you want to know?" Sheila asked one final time.

"*Yes!*" Sarah, both mothers, and I answered in unison.

"Okay, it's a baby boy!" she said. Within seconds, the tears were streaming. Both mothers were crying, while Sarah and I hugged. I was carrying our son. I'd always dreamed of having a boy.

"Are you totally sure it's a boy?" I asked through tears of joy.

"Absolutely," she said, pointing to the area on the screen that left no doubt.

With that news, I climbed off the table, dressed myself, and prepared to find out what Sarah was carrying. I had no regrets. My son would be registered for blue blankets and baby caps. His bedding would feature images of cars, superheroes, and sports figures. I'd never thought I would gender-stereotype my baby, but within seconds of finding out I was having a boy, my every thought was in the color blue.

Now it was finally Sarah's turn. She had hoped for a girl, and now that we knew I was having our boy, I hoped for a little girl, too. Up until that day, I'd only cared about the babies' health. But now that we were here on the table, able to count fingers and toes, see hearts beat and make sure lungs were developing, hey, why not become invested in the outcome?

"Sheila, tell us it's a girl!" I said through my hormonal laughter.

She frowned. "This baby's a stubborn thing; I can't get a good angle. Sarah, can you cough? Maybe that will help move the baby so I can get a better view." She pushed down on Sarah's belly with the sonogram wand.

"Is everything okay?" Sarah asked nervously.

Sheila reassured us. "Everything looks fine. Ten fingers. Ten toes. Strong heartbeat. Lungs are developing just right. This is a totally healthy baby. I just can't tell if it's a boy or a girl. I'm really sorry, Sarah."

"You mean you're done? You can't find out?" Sarah asked, her voice starting to quiver.

"We will definitely be able to tell at your next sonogram . . . next month," Sheila said apologetically.

"Did you say *next month*?" Sarah shouted. "Kristen, who didn't want to know what she was having, is leaving here today knowing she is having a boy? Now I've got an office full of people who have placed bets on what I am carrying, and *we won't know until next month*?"

This was not how the day's story was supposed to go. The appointment was to end with Sarah being told she was carrying a healthy baby girl. Instead, she was left in limbo and I was unable to enjoy the news that I did not even know I wanted. Well, that's not *entirely* true: Inside, I was dancing and shouting the whole way home. I was carrying our little baby boy!

Sarah

It was time for the baby showers and our phone was ringing non-stop. Our mothers were acting as if these were the weddings they'd never get to plan for us. Each mother wanted to throw her own event and carefully select the guest list, menus, and invitations. My mother wanted a small intimate family party at her house, while Kristen's mother, Jeanne, reserved an entire restaurant and invited friends of friends; no one was left off the list. My mother's friends—a tight-knit group of ladies who'd been close for years—wanted to throw us a shower, too. With three showers barreling down on me, I'd come face-to-face with the most dreaded part of my pregnancy: registering.

I'm a girl who likes things: clothes, accessories, home furnishings, you name it. But registering for twins intimidated me. There was so much bright plastic stuff to go through. And did we really need two of everything? Despite my trepidation, off to Babies "R" Us we went. Soon enough, we were armed with a scanner gun and directed to tag all the items we needed for our pending bundles of joy. I started firing away: two car seats, two bouncy seats, a double stroller, a single stroller, bottles, and onesies. Then I completely shut down. The thrill of shooting things with the scanner gun wore off quickly; I was overwhelmed and rendered useless in the middle of the store.

Fortunately, Kristen's sister-in-law, Klio, who was the mother of a one-year-old, had joined us for the registry process. Klio grabbed the scanner gun and marched through the aisles, clicking away. "You need this, you need this, you need this, you don't need this, you don't need this . . ." On and on she went as I followed her like an obedient child, more than happy to relinquish control of the registry to my two personal shoppers.

I had initially looked forward to our registry day like a child anticipating Christmas, but now, Kristen was the "registry expert," having taken control of the entire project since she knew what she was carrying. It wasn't fair: I was twenty-three weeks pregnant and still in limbo. I tried in vain to enjoy the process of picking things out for our son and his mystery-gendered sibling, but I could not mentally commit to the baby registry process; I needed to know the sex of the baby I was carrying. I watched as Kristen and Klio feverishly checked items off our list: two Pack 'n Plays, two cribs, two swings, two mattresses, two changing tables.

"I love the sailboat bumpers for his crib, don't you?" Kristen asked with excitement. "And look how cute this gender-neutral ladybug set is." She was trying to comfort me, but her carefully chosen words sent me into a tailspin.

"Just enjoy yourself," I said, secretly imploring her to deal with the process on her own. I plopped myself down on a glider chair and closed my eyes.

"Is it comfortable?" Kristen asked. "Should we scan it for the registry?"

Kristen *loved* the registry: It became her new favorite pastime. Every day, she would log on from home, adding new items and removing things she no longer wanted. Regrettably, I'd given her the highly acclaimed *Baby Bargains* book, a guide that does extensive reviews of current baby products. It served only to fuel her passion further. She compared car seats for safety and value, high chairs for space and efficiency, and strollers for city streets versus country roads. The item that thwarted her most, though, was the baby glider, and now that I was sitting in one, she made a last-ditch effort to draw me into the day's events.

"We just won't know which one is right until we've had a chance to really *relax* in one," she said, staring at me and the chair almost obsessively.

"Stop trying to include me!" I shouted.

* * *

During the monthlong wait to find out my baby's gender—a period we eventually referred to as "Gender-gate"—our lives became physically challenging. Two pregnant women sharing a studio apartment and crammed into a double bed night after night began to take its toll. On the advice of a friend, we went to Bed, Bath and Beyond to purchase body pillows. Kristen waited in the car while I wrestled four of these aptly named body pillows into my shopping cart. Five feet long and stuffed with down feathers, the pillows kept popping out of my cart as I fought my way down the aisle. Most pregnant women need only one enormous body pillow to get them through a pregnancy. Due to our unique situation, we each needed a pillow. And because we were now living between two residences, our studio apartment and our house on Long Island, it made the most sense to have body pillows at both places.

By the time I made it to the checkout counter, exhausted and out of breath, the clerk peered over the mountain of pillows between us and asked, "Are we having a sale?"

"You would not believe me if I told you," I replied. "And no. You are not having a sale."

He rang up our three hundred and seventy five dollars' worth of body pillows and I was on my way. As I struggled through the exit door to the waiting car, I could see Kristen blowing her nose. Upon entering the car, the radio was blasting a familiar song. In fact, it was a song I knew Kristen disliked very much. So to hear it playing at such a loud volume alarmed me.

"Are you crying?" I asked Kristen as she wiped her face with a Dunkin' Donuts napkin.

"I've just never listened to the words of this song before. Have you?" Kristen could hardly get the words out. "I mean, our babies," she sobbed, "I hope they daaaaaance . . ." She continued to sniffle, blow her nose, and sing the words to "I Hope You Dance" by Lee Ann Womack while I stuffed the pillows into the car.

"Do you need me to drive?" I asked when I returned to the front seat, exhausted and out of breath. Kristen's second-trimester hormonal imbalance had reached a new low. It was as if she was drunk or on drugs. I no longer felt safe with her driving. The fits of laughter were one thing, but now there were bouts of crying over anything related to children, babies, puppies, kittens, or grandparents. Even the feel-good segments on the *Today* show resulted in fits of hysterical sobbing for Kristen. I could no longer navigate my way through her maze of emotions.

"The 'I Hope You Dance' song does not make you cry?" Kristen asked, pushing me. "What are you, a robot?"

"No, I'm not a robot—I'm stable!"

"Are you annoyed because I know what I am having and you still have to wait three more weeks to find out?" she said. She was sure this was the answer to why the "I Hope You Dance" song did not make me cry.

"Kristen!" I said, exasperated. "I don't cry to that song. I have *never* cried to that song. And the reason I do not cry to that song is because I am not hormonally imbalanced. Are you? Do we need to talk to Dr. Rosenbaum about you having postpartum depression? This family cannot afford to be one man down after these babies are born!" Now I was completely panicked; I hadn't thought about what would happen if anything actually went wrong.

"Maybe crying to that song is a pregnant thing," Kristen said, unable to resist mocking me. I sighed and looked out the window. We were going to have a few long months ahead of us.

Chapter 10

A Whole New You

Sarah

The day of my twenty-four-week sonogram, I woke up a jangle of nerves. I'd been living each day only to get to this appointment. Like every good mother-to-be, I kept telling myself, "I just want this baby to be healthy; that's all that matters." But I couldn't deny what I felt deep down: I wanted a girl.

"You need to stop worrying; we're going to have what we're going to have," Kristen said as we got ready to leave the apartment.

"What if she can't tell, again? I can't go on like this."

"She'll be able to tell—*let's go*," Kristen said.

When we got to our doctor's office, I practically undressed myself in the reception area. There was no small talk; Sheila got right down to business. Slathering my stomach with jelly, she immediately began to search for the clue that would end my agony.

"Well, that was easy," she said, looking at the screen.

"What?" Kristen and I cried. "Tell us!"

"It's a girl!" she said.

"*Yes!*" Kristen said, making a little fist-pump. "Pink and blue!"

"Are you sure?" I asked.

"Completely positive," Sheila said.

"But I've heard so many stories of women being told they're having a girl; then they deliver the baby and it's a boy."

"This is most definitely a little girl," Sheila said, laughing. "C'mon, you're going to give her a complex."

After all this struggle and heartache and waiting, I was going to give birth to a little girl. I asked Sheila to confirm the news at least another three times. I had wanted so badly to hear those words, and when I finally did, I couldn't believe them.

"You guys are so lucky," Sheila said as I got dressed. "A boy and a girl!"

As soon as Kristen and I stepped out the front door of Dr. Rosenbaum's office, I called my mother to tell her the news. Immediately, she started bawling. Her own mother had always told her, "You always want to have a girl, because a girl will never leave you." She already had two grandsons and another one on the way. So this was her one and only granddaughter.

"I want to give you the baby bracelet you wore on your wrist when you were a baby," she said between sniffles. "And your hand-knit ponchos I still have, and your pink baby blanket . . ." She listed all the items she'd held on to with the dream of having a granddaughter. I hung up the phone and wiped away a tear as I turned to Kristen.

"Just so you know, if this turns out to be a boy, I'll be okay with that," I said.

"You are out of your mind!" she said. We laughed and hailed a cab. I was unable to stop smiling.

By the third trimester, the novelty of our dual pregnancies had worn off. We were safe from miscarriages, I was officially carrying the girl I had dreamed of, and we'd been showered with enough gifts to open our own department store. We even had our "just-in-cases" ready, Kristen's nickname for our packed hospital bags. The only thing left to do was to be uncomfortable. And that's exactly what we were. You name the pregnancy side effect and one of us suffered from it acutely: hemorrhoids, carpal tunnel syndrome, varicose veins, heartburn, swollen ankles, bleeding gums, constipation, and nosebleeds. By the third trimester, we weren't doing anything halfway.

One night, we had just returned to our house on Long Island after dinner with family when Kristen dropped the keys to the front door and inadvertently kicked them deep under the front porch. I threw my arms up in the air.

"Call the locksmith!" I said, exasperated at the thought of having to bend over.

"Just hoist me through the front window," Kristen said, unable to reach far enough to get the keys herself. We both stood uselessly in front of the porch. I pictured our neighbors, Janet and Mike, peering out their kitchen window across the street as I shoved Kristen through the window, Winnie-the-Pooh-like. "Hey, wait a minute," Kristen said. "If we call a locksmith to change the locks, couldn't he just grab the keys under the porch instead?"

I rubbed my forehead and said, "You make an excellent point. I guess it takes two women with 'baby brain' to come up with one obvious idea."

Kristen headed toward our neighbor Mike's side door. I could hear Tucker barking in our foyer, aware of his owners' return and eager to be let out into the front yard for relief. I plopped down on the stoop and crossed my legs, in need of the very same relief Tucker was waiting for. Kristen returned with Mike in tow.

"What have you ladies gotten yourselves into now?" he asked as he leaned down, pointing a flashlight under the porch.

"Thank you, Mike," we said in unison as he handed us the keys.

In our family, Mike was known as the block husband. On the weekdays Kristen and I stayed on Long Island, I commuted into the city with him. Mike and Janet's five-year-old daughter, Lily, was earmarked as our future babysitter. Since he had no son of his own,

Mike often told us he looked forward to playing baseball and football with our little boy. We were relieved that such a wonderful male influence lived only steps away from our home.

In our city apartment, the combination of pregnant bellies, body pillows, and Tucker the puppy in our bed led to the forced eviction of one of us. That person happened to be me. I volunteered to sleep on the love seat in our studio apartment for one reason: If I didn't, Kristen would rightfully insist we stay at our Long Island house. And that would mean I had to commute into the city for work every day—my worst nightmare. So every night at bedtime I pretended to love sleeping on our sofa. I even went so far as to claim I preferred it to our bed. "It's so much better for my back," I said as I stiffly turned over. So while I lay awake in discomfort, suffering from the worst case of pregnancy insomnia ever known, Kristen snuggled up with her body pillow and our puppy in our fluffy double bed, drifting off to a perfect night's sleep. Eventually I would fall asleep, too, only to be woken by the sound of our bathroom toilet being flushed.

"Must you do that at three A.M.?" I'd inquire through clenched teeth.

"It's rude not to flush the toilet," Kristen would reply as she staggered back into our bed, half-asleep.

"I implore you to reverse your thinking on this," I would say, now wide awake. "It is ruder to wake a pregnant woman suffering from insomnia and sleeping on a love seat sofa than it is to leave a toilet unflushed." Then I'd stare at the ceiling, seething, for another two hours until it was time to get up for work.

Soon, Kristen and I were so physically big that when we tried to hug we couldn't even get our arms around each other. We must have looked ridiculous. Sex brought up a whole other set of challenges. We would climb into bed at night with every intention of being intimate, but with our big bellies, multiple pregnancy ailments, and sheer exhaustion, we would soon quit. "On the inside, I want to be with you," Kristen would mumble. Then we would roll over and snuggle with our individual body pillows.

But we also had dozens of sweet moments. We loved to press our bellies together so the babies could commune with each other, and it often even stimulated them to move. Many a night, Kristen and I sat on the couch, rubbing each other's feet; then at some point we just couldn't reach them any longer. Trips to buy maternity clothes were always good for a laugh. We would cram ourselves into one dressing room, until one of us would have to waddle out to get different sizes. During that third trimester, our family motto was, "Every woman for herself." It was survival of the fittest—actually, make that survival of the *fattest*.

Our trips around town to local stores began to draw quite a bit of attention. Most pregnant women are treated with courtesy by store employees and fellow shoppers. But two extremely pregnant women who are obviously shopping together draw even more attention to themselves.

"Wow, how fun, pregnant friends!" people would say.

Others would ask, "Did your husbands know you planned to get pregnant at the same time?"

Or even better: "Pregnant sisters?"

I loved answering the unsuspecting question-askers. "We're partners, not sisters," I'd bluntly reply. In New York City, most people realized I did not mean business partners, but in our small town, I wanted to make sure they completely understood, so I would add, "Not business partners—life partners."

Kristen, meanwhile, would busy herself in a nearby aisle. She refused to come out of hiding until she felt sure the people I was talking to were open to our situation. Then it was her turn to mortify *me*: She'd chime in with details about water retention, swollen ankles, or the fact that she hadn't seen her feet in months, sharing this information with the FedEx man, the neighborhood dog walker, or the Salvation Army coin collector who parked herself on our corner. But hey, at least she was talking.

Privately, I worried about Kristen's comfort level when it came to revealing our story. She reserved the whole of it for those who looked liberal and were under forty. If we planned to successfully rear two children through well-adjusted childhoods, *both* of their moms had to get the message straight: Same-sex-parented families were just like any other. I warned her that once both babies were here, she'd have no choice but to tell our story to everyone, including sixty-year-old men in plaid pants who played golf with her Republican father and uncles. She would half-jokingly say that she was looking forward to the challenge, but I was serious. These babies were not going to be taught to hide or be ashamed of where they came from. And it was up to the two of us to make sure they were not.

One night, we went to our favorite Mexican restaurant to have dinner. It was cold outside, but we were warm and cozy as we watched the waiter prepare homemade guacamole at our table. As we started to dig into a basket of chips, Kristen looked me in the eyes and said, "Thank you for making this possible."

"You know I'm happy to come here whenever," I said.

She smiled at the ceiling. "Not this," she said. Then she gestured to her belly. "*This*. I never could have done it without someone pushing me to do it, not to mention having the financial support. You've given me such a gift."

I was already emotional at that stage of my pregnancy, but hearing those words from the woman who was carrying the second half of our set of twins nearly sent me into convulsions of tears. "Well, you're the best gift *I've* ever gotten," I said. "This is everything I've ever dreamed of."

We raised our glasses of sparkling water and toasted our good fortune.

Kristen

When I was six months pregnant, the band opened for Joan Jett and the Blackhearts at the Community Theater in Morristown, New Jersey. I was self-conscious to be onstage and showing, but the crowd was warm and receptive. As I stepped up to the mic to sing my lines, I noticed a sensation I'd never had before: My hands were numb. I could not feel a thing. Between songs, I would shake them repeatedly, but they were sound asleep. "Pregnancy-induced carpal tunnel syndrome" was the diagnosis of overwhelming public opinion. Suddenly, every pregnant woman who came before me said she'd experienced it too and had great sympathy for my situation—except for Sarah, of course. She was the only pregnant woman in the history of pregnant women to not share a single pregnancy-induced side effect with me. Instead, she suffered from one half of all the possible pregnancy side effects and I suffered from the other half. Restless-leg syndrome was Sarah's issue. Lower-back pain was mine. Migraine headaches landed in Sarah's column, while extreme water retention fell into mine.

"Do you have stool softener?" Sarah asked at the pharmacy the day we went shopping for all our pregnancy-related side effect needs.

"And Depends?" Sarah also had laughter-induced bladder-control issues.

"Is there anything else I can help you with?" the pharmacist asked, glancing at his teenage clerk.

"As a matter of fact, yes," Sarah said. "She's got two numb hands and I need something to support the varicose veins in my legs. Oh, and hemorrhoids—what would you recommend for those?"

The pharmacist grabbed two wrist braces and a box of Tucks. "Anything else?" he asked.

"Yes, actually, there is," Sarah said, rubbing her chest. "I need something for this awful heartburn I've got."

"How do you know when you have heartburn?" I asked as a small burp escaped me. "Excuse me."

"You burp your food up," Sarah said.

"Aha!" I said. "It seems we have two things in common." Leaning into the counter, I half-whispered, "I need Tucks, too." When we left, Sarah said I'd seemed embarrassed. "I have to be proud to come out about my hemorrhoids, too?" I joked.

The wrist braces soon became a new toy for Tucker to chew on. Running after a thirteen-pound puppy while seven months pregnant was not how I'd pictured incorporating cardio into my daily program. Sarah and I found ourselves blaming each other on a regular basis for leaving the carpal tunnel braces within Tucker's reach. I'd run one way, Sarah would run the other, and eventually we would corner poor Tucker and retrieve the chewed-up braces. These were the things no one could have warned us about when we both got pregnant at the same time. And thank goodness they didn't.

Chapter 11

Natural Woman

Sarah

As the third trimester wore on, it finally dawned on me that this baby inside me would somehow have to get out. I was scared to death of delivery. *Petrified* is more like it. Even at birth, babies, I knew, were much bigger than the birth canal. My mind couldn't comprehend how an infant could pass through *that area* without excruciating pain. If I'd thought about it for too long when I'd started the process, I would never have allowed myself to get pregnant. I'd been able to ignore this truth for much of the first and second trimesters, but the reality was now all too apparent.

Kristen's therapist, whom she started seeing weekly to prepare herself for same-sex parenthood, planted the "doula seed" in her head. A doula attends to the emotional and physical comfort of laboring women. They do not provide medical support but they offer suggestions and alternatives to help the laboring mother deliver naturally. Perhaps not surprisingly, Kristen was totally into this idea, while I was firmly on the fence. From the moment I found out I was pregnant, my primary concern was pain management. So to voluntarily invite a proponent of an au naturel birth into my delivery room felt downright risky. With our due dates looming so close together, there was no guarantee either of us would be available for the other. Our mothers volunteered to help in our respective delivery rooms, but it was a proposition neither of us could fathom. Kristen's mother turned every event into a social gathering, so upon offering her services she began inviting cousins and siblings into the delivery room with her. She was clearly well-intentioned but was not going to be the right coach for the job. And my mother was far too opinionated and emotionally charged about the birth to provide the calm detachment we needed. So we agreed that a doula would become our second-in-command, and the one we chose happened to be a childhood friend of Kristen's: Jen, the redheaded former lead singer of No Comment, Kristen's first band. I was baffled by my partner's lack of bashfulness.

"You're really comfortable with Jen seeing you deliver a baby?" I asked.

"If you had a choice, wouldn't you rather have an old friend in the delivery room than someone you hardly knew?" Kristen asked.

"No, I would not," I said. "So in fact, this situation works out: You get to have a doula you've known for years, and I get to have one I am just meeting for the first time."

Jen's first duty was to come up with our pregnancy contingency plan. We would need a backup doula if we both went into labor at the same time. We would also need a third doula on call, just in case we both went into labor at the same time and one of the first two doulas ran into an emergency situation and could not make it to the hospital.

"Two days ago, I didn't even know what a doula was," I joked. "Now every doula in the Northeast is on call for my labor!"

Kristen looked at me with a flat stare. "Sarah, there are more than three doulas in the Northeast." Now that she knew her former lead singer was a doula, she was the authority on all things natural birth related.

Jen's "doula package" came with private labor and delivery classes. I was not interested in the classes and asked Kristen if I could skip them. After all, I planned to rely heavily on modern medicine to get me through my birth experience. I felt the only thing I needed from a birthing class was to know the proper positioning so an anesthesiologist could quickly and efficiently insert an epidural into my spine.

Kristen

Once my friend Jen was on board as our doula, I started to get very excited about giving birth. I began reading books and watching videos to prepare myself for as natural a birth experience as possible. I found myself reading into the late hours of the night—not because I was suffering from insomnia, but because I wanted to learn as much as I could before I was wheeled into the delivery room. I believed that the more I knew, the more control I would have over my body and my baby's birth. I would try in earnest to share my findings with Sarah, who was often awake with me during the night, suffering from insomnia.

"Sarah, look: These people created a birthing environment called the Farm, where family members, friends, and midwives all help each other deliver babies naturally!" I said. The thought of having no medical intervention was very appealing to me and I admired these women for having the courage to give birth in an organic setting, miles away from any hospital.

"I am looking forward to going to the Epidural Farm," she mumbled, rolling over and putting a pillow over her head in an attempt to get some sleep.

At such a late stage in my own pregnancy, I had no intention of rewriting my birth plan. I still intended to use my Western doctors and my hospital, with its pediatric neonatal intensive care unit steps away. But I also planned to use as many natural techniques as possible, while holding off on medication for as long as my body could tolerate.

The more I brought it up, the more Sarah would plead, "Please, I'm begging you! I cannot talk about this!"

This, of course, cracked me up. My partner loved to brag about all the varsity sports she'd played as a teenager, even describing herself as a "feminine lesbian with a rugged edge." The "rugged edge" part always got me: Let's just say Sarah likes to hire out for her dirty work. Had she been able to pay someone to push the baby out for her, I knew she would have. But she also harbored an intensely competitive side. And that's the side I played to when I tried to convince her to go the doula route: "If you were *really* rugged—like, as rugged as I am," I would say, "you would push this baby out naturally. You would at least attend the birthing classes Jen is offering." I knew she wouldn't be able to resist the challenge. Eventually, she relented and agreed to participate in the birthing classes.

She did so under two conditions: "One, you cannot judge me for wanting immediate medical intervention upon going into labor," she said. She was vehement on this point and I agreed with her. I saw no reason to make her do anything that would make her uncomfortable during the birth of our child. She continued. "And you *cannot* force me to watch any videos of women giving birth!" That one I agreed to with my fingers crossed behind my back: I knew full well that when it came time to watch a birthing video in class, I would make her look.

"You've got yourself a deal," I said. And we shook hands.

I was excited for our first class to start. Doula Jen, as Sarah had nicknamed her, arrived at our house to find one overeager student with freshly sharpened pencils and a crisp new notepad. I planned to score an A+ on my final exam. Sarah, on the other hand, was nervous and distracted. She somehow managed to work the word "epidural" into every sentence she uttered.

"I have no problem with any of this as long as I have an epidural hooked up as soon I enter the hospital," Sarah said, speaking up even in the most irrelevant places.

"Actually, I was really just reminding you to pack your own slippers," Doula Jen said. "You may feel more comfortable getting around the maternity ward in your own things after giving birth."

"Oh. Yes. I agree. I would probably prefer my own slippers," Sarah replied, adding, "With an epidural."

Doula Jen knew full well she had two very different students on her hands. To avoid scaring Sarah, she spoke of slippers and other necessities for the hospital. She knew talk of babies' take-home outfits would set her at ease. And it worked: After a quick bathroom break, Doula Jen slipped her "kid gloves" back on and delicately began discussing our next topic: the first signs of labor. She reviewed what it might be like when our water broke and what an early contraction would feel like. We were instructed always to call our doctor first, and then her. We discussed different scenarios of how the earlier part of the labor might take place. We could remain at home after our water broke—the option I preferred—or we could head straight into the hospital at the very first sign of labor. This was the approach Sarah favored. In fact, Sarah's knee-jerk response to every single thing Jen said was, "Will it hurt?"

"I can't lie to you, Sarah," Doula Jen said in a tone that could have put the most frightened patient at ease. "At some point during labor, with or without the epidural, it will probably hurt." Doula Jen made herself clear: It would be her personal mission to make sure Sarah received whatever she needed to have a successful, pain-managed delivery. We spent a majority of our first class focused on Sarah's worries and concerns. Most couples taking a class have only one pregnant person among them, so focusing on the pregnant partner's worries would make perfect sense. But we weren't other couples. I was just as pregnant as the worried partner and I was ready to cut to the good stuff. I needed some hands-on expertise about how I was getting my baby out with as little drug intervention as possible.

"So, Kristen," Doula Jen said, "I think we will spend the first several hours of your labor at home. I will have you riding the birthing ball to help expedite your cervix's dilation." Doula Jen rolled the birthing ball into the center of the room and gave me a demonstration of what I should do.

Sarah watched. "So, I won't need to do that?" she asked.

"I don't think so, Sarah," Doula Jen replied. "We will probably have you in a hospital bed at this point of your labor. We will have you as comfortable as possible in a reclined position." I rolled back and forth on the birthing ball, asking Doula Jen if I was doing it correctly. "That's perfect, Kristen. Can you feel how your pelvis is able to expand while you roll forward? This will really help as you're trying to get that cervix open and ready for delivery."

"So I don't get to do that, too?" Sarah inquired.

"You really can't roll around on the ball when you are hooked up to a spinal epidural," Doula Jen explained. "You will need to be lying down on the bed."

After the birthing ball demonstration, we moved on to watching an educational video. It was a documentary movie that demonstrated a woman having a completely natural labor, with no medical intervention at all. Sarah warned Doula Jen in advance, "Don't expect me to be able to watch this. I'm not even sure I want the audio turned up." I, on the other hand, was watching with pen poised, ready to take it all in. I had read a lot about the pros of a completely drug-free delivery. I knew the statistics and how drug-induced labors were more likely to lead to cesarean births, something I was eager to avoid. Sarah, on the other hand, was being exposed to this information for the first time. Despite the many attempts I'd made to have a conversation with her about what I was learning in the books, she'd refused to listen. She was simply not ready to hear what I had to say.

But now she sat on our sofa, her mouth agape. We had just seen a woman push a baby out with no epidural or pain medication involved. And Sarah watched the whole thing, from start to finish, without covering her eyes. The woman in the film was an average person. She was in her late thirties and this was her first pregnancy. She was not an Olympic athlete or a marathon runner. She was not in her early twenties, as Sarah assumed someone had to be in order to endure a natural labor. As a matter of fact, the woman in the film looked like she could be either one of us. By the time the closing credits rolled, Sarah's competitive drive had been activated, and it seemed she was ready to rumble. Sarah spoke half a thought out loud: "If that woman can do it . . ."

"Are you serious?" I laughed. She was ready to move her entire birth process out of a hospital and into a birthing center equipped with nothing but love and incense. I shook my head in utter disbelief.

"I can do this!" she proclaimed.

During this time, the band was playing sporadic dates with different lead singers to see if any would stick. In December, when I was eight and a half months pregnant, we played at our old haunt, the Bitter End in New York City. It was a great night, but I wondered if we'd ever play another show after the babies were born. My bandmates had been forced to find part-time jobs to make ends meet. It was hard enough to come back after losing our lead singer; my pregnancy made us do it at a snail's pace. Our bass player, Jen Z., lived in Philadelphia and was finding it difficult to travel to New York for rehearsals, since she was working side jobs and trying to get pregnant herself. She eventually did get pregnant and never rejoined the band. Things felt like they were coming undone for us, but I didn't have time to fall apart as well. I was too busy planning for our babies' impending arrival.

Sarah

I entered the doctor's office ready to map out my new birthing strategy. Kristen had convinced me I should still deliver in the hospital, but I wanted to make it perfectly clear to Dr. Rosenbaum that I would not be rushed through my process. I felt empowered now that I was aware of my options. As Dr. Rosenbaum entered the room, I prepared to tell her my news. Before I could get the first words out she said, "So, Sarah, based on this latest sonogram, it looks like the baby is in a transverse position. She's not in danger, but she is lying sideways across your abdomen. We are going to need to schedule a C-section. How does February fourth sound to you?"

I was totally caught off guard. That was *not* what I expected to hear at my appointment. I had only just come around to the idea of a natural labor, and now that I had, both my heart and my mind were set on it. "Is she breech?" I asked, having heard the term before, though I wasn't quite sure what it meant.

"No. Transverse is not the same as breech, but it is similar in the sense that you cannot have a vaginal delivery," explained Dr. Rosenbaum. "So we will just go in there on the fourth and take her out safely."

Dr. Rosenbaum was talking to the "old Sarah," the one she assumed wanted nothing to do with natural childbirth. The Sarah who had offered to pay extra to schedule a C-section up front the minute she found out she was pregnant. So what I said next really surprised her: "Is there nothing we can do to change this situation? I was really looking forward to pushing this baby out!"

Dr. Rosenbaum, now confused, glanced down at her notes. "Was it Kristen who has been pushing for pain meds and a C-section all this time?" she said, flipping the pages of her file. Eventually, she looked up at me.

"No, no," I said. "I did want to talk to you about that today. I took a class with my doula, and I've had a change of heart. I really want to try to deliver this baby with very little medical intervention."

Dr. Rosenbaum removed her glasses and placed both hands on her desk. "Sarah, this baby is in a transverse position. You are thirty-six weeks pregnant. The chances of her moving into the proper position to allow for a vaginal delivery are slight. We can hope for the best, but plan for a C-section on February fourth. I'm sorry."

I left the appointment distraught. As soon as I got home, I called Doula Jen to let her know that I would no longer need her services. "Don't throw in the towel just yet," she said. She knew an acupuncturist in the city who'd had remarkably favorable results helping transverse babies turn into the proper head-first position for delivery. I was willing to try.

The acupuncturist was a block away from our apartment but had no available appointments for weeks. "I don't have weeks to wait!" I cried in frustration. When I explained my situation she agreed to see me that night, after her regular office hours.

Grateful, I arrived at her office and explained my whole story: how I'd hoped for a C-section through most of my pregnancy, but now that the time was here, I wanted to experience the birth of my child. The news of her transverse position had me and my entire family worried. The doctor downplayed the diagnosis, but Kristen and I had read terrible things online and felt we had reason to be fearful. If my water broke while the baby was sideways, her umbilical cord could come out first and be compressed, which could be a fatal situation if I could not get to a hospital immediately. "I have an extremely high success rate with transverse babies," the acupuncturist told me. "So long as you keep an open mind and follow my orders, I'm sure the baby will move into the proper position." This type of Eastern approach was much more in keeping with Kristen's thinking than mine—and the thought of being stuck like a pincushion was causing me major anxiety—but I didn't want the woman to sense my hesitation. I took a few deep breaths, channeled Kristen, and told her I was an open vessel.

The therapist lit some candles and led me to a table. She told me to remove my shoes and began massaging my feet. I was totally caught off guard by this, as I assumed I was there to get stuck with needles. Seeing my confusion she explained, "We don't use needles

for this form of therapy. I'm sorry; I assumed your doula explained."
It was very likely Doula Jen had explained this to me, but my brain
was hardwired to hear "acupuncture" and expect needles.

"Moxibustion is a therapy that uses a Chinese herb called moxa,"
she said. "I burn a stick of the herb close to acupuncture points in
your foot to help stimulate circulation. It will help your baby move
into position." I didn't believe a single word of it, but the foot massage was fantastic. I arrived home after the appointment reeking of
moxa. I had already begun mentally preparing myself for a C-section
when Kristen started grilling me for every detail of my session with
the acupuncturist.

"She burned a candle on my toe and expects this baby to flip
around into the correct position," I said, making it clear that I had
no faith in the procedure whatsoever. "And you have to do it to me
every night for the next two weeks, by the way."

By the following night, I had completely forgotten about my
moxibustion therapy. I was too busy being grumpy about my pending C-section. "Where are those candles we have to burn?" Kristen
asked, still fully invested in the moxibustion process.

I pulled the partially burned candle from the bag and handed it to
her, saying insistently, "The foot rub is the most critical part of the
therapy." Kristen did not fall for it. She had already looked up moxibustion therapy online and knew exactly what she was supposed to
do. She lit the candle and began twirling it around my toes as I read
the latest issue of *People* magazine.

"This stuff smells *really* strong," Kristen said, surprised. Then she
added, "Whoa! This baby is really moving around inside me!"

Suddenly, we were hit with an unpleasant realization: If the smell
of the moxa herb was going to work to move my baby into the correct position, couldn't it also move Kristen's baby *out* of position?
"Blow that thing out!" I shouted. The last thing we needed was to
"moxibust" Kristen's properly positioned baby out of place. The
smell from the therapy lingered in our apartment for hours. If I was

going to continue with this procedure on a nightly basis, Kristen was going to have to leave the apartment for several hours so as not to be affected by it.

The following two nights, Kristen busied herself in the evenings so I could perform my moxibustion ritual. By the third night, I had given up. We were headed out to Long Island for the weekend and I intentionally left my candles behind. Kristen could not understand my lack of faith in the process, but it seemed obvious to me. Burning a candle that smelled like marijuana around my toe was going to do nothing more than make our apartment stink. I was resigned to it. The scheduled C-section I had so desperately wanted in the beginning had become my reality. And the procedure was less than a week away.

Kristen

In late January, I was nine months pregnant. I'd just finished wishing my father a happy birthday on the phone and was now sitting at my desk with a peanut butter and jelly sandwich, reading e-mails. A message from my lawyer friend Rikki popped up on my screen. She had marked it urgent, so I opened it right away. In the e-mail, Rikki wrote that effective immediately, New York State would allow same-sex couples to list both their names on a birth certificate if they were legally married. Of course, it was still not legal for us to get married in New York State. But the state would grant us certain rights if we got married in one of the few states that *did* recognize same-sex marriage. I whipped around to share the exciting news with my old friend Lizzy—the one who'd offered to take care of us during the final weeks of our pregnancies.

The night before, she'd arrived on our doorstep from Los Angeles to help us do all the things that a nonpregnant partner would do: bend down to pick things up, lift items, make dinner, walk the dog. But with the news of New York State possibly allowing us to put both our names on our children's birth certificates, Lizzy's first order of business became figuring out how to get us married.

"We can do this in Connecticut," she announced from behind her laptop computer. "And we can have it done by Monday." After some online research, Lizzy discovered it would take one full business day for the marriage license to take effect. If she and I drove to Connecticut the following day, we could fill out the paperwork, pay the fee, and by Monday morning Sarah and I could take our vows.

Traveling at this stage in my pregnancy seemed risky. But suddenly, the right to list both our names on a piece of paper took precedence over everything. Whether or not it would hold up in a court outside New York was debatable, but our children deserved to have both parents listed on their birth certificates. Our shotgun wedding would take place in seventy-two hours, as long as neither of us went into labor over the weekend.

The following day, as Lizzy and I drove home from our adventure, I called my mother. I couldn't wait to share the news with her. "Sarah and I will have a legal marriage license by Monday!" I exclaimed. The more I thought about it, the more excited I got.

"That is fantastic, Kristen! Why do you have to go all the way to Connecticut? Can't you just do it here in New York?" She was as thrilled as she was confused.

I tried my best to clarify. "No, Mom. It is not legal for us to get married in New York State yet. But if we get married in a state where same-sex marriage is legal, New York will allow us to list both our names on the babies' birth certificates." The more I explained it, the more my mother's maternal instinct kicked in.

"New York State is going to make you and Sarah travel all the way to Connecticut just so you can have your names on your own babies' birth certificates? What type of ridiculous law is that?" It seemed clear that at least some of my grandmother's liberal leanings had been passed down through the generations.

"Mom . . ." I tried interrupting, but she continued on.

"You're *both* nine months pregnant; you need to be able to get married in your own state!" She sounded incensed.

"I know, Mom, but this is actually really good news. So please be excited for us, and tell Dad that Sarah and I are getting married on Monday." By the time I hung up the phone, she was completely on board and excited for the event.

The press release went out via my mother in the form of a phone chain: "Kristen and Sarah are getting married on Monday!" she told every single person she knew. Soon, I'd been informed that my brother, Tom; his wife; and his daughter all planned to witness the nuptials. My sister, Cathy, would drive the band's tour van to accommodate everyone who wanted to attend. Even Cousin Kelly would keep her daughter home from school that day so they could take the drive with us. As soon as I found this out, I called my mother and begged her not to turn this into the event of the century. All Sarah and I needed was a ride to Connecticut, a legal marriage document, and a justice of the peace. Then we could relax during our final weeks of pregnancy, knowing our affairs were in order. I thought that I had made it clear that we had no intention of inviting our families along.

"Of course, Kristen, I understand. But you can't expect your family not to be there," my mom pleaded.

"Yes I can, Mom. I love you all, but I cannot have this turn into a fifty-phone-call event."

"Oh, Kristen, don't be ridiculous. I made one call to Sarah's mother. She is looking into restaurants in the area that can accommodate our party for a luncheon following the ceremony. We are taking care of it all."

"Sarah's mother? We haven't even told her we're getting married yet!" I shrieked.

"She knows now," my mother said calmly. "And so does her brother, Spencer, and his wife, Maura. They plan to keep the boys home from school that day to join us. In fact, her whole family has made plans to join us on Monday. I thought you'd be happy about that!"

And so, our shotgun wedding, less than twelve hours in the making, turned into a confirmed fifty-guest affair, complete with a three-course sit-down luncheon, maids of honor, speeches, and gifts. All of our siblings, cousins, and even some friends planned on joining the cavalcade to Connecticut. Except for one thing: Sarah had no idea that while she was at work that day, Project Birth Certificate had turned into the wedding event of the season. She was about to find out.

Sarah

There is a hormone that goes off in a woman when she is two weeks away from her due date. Doubly present in our household, this hormone was directing us to cross our "t"s and dot our "i"s. Kristen and I had been together nearly four years, and from the moment we'd started dating, we'd finished each other's every thought. Since we were always in lockstep, I thought she felt the same way about our pending shotgun nuptials: We needed this marriage certificate to protect our family. The romantic wedding of our dreams, the one we spoke of and envisioned for ourselves, would come once New York State officially legalized gay marriage. I had been conditioned by my job at *Real Simple* to take deadlines very seriously. Now, with the two biggest deadlines of my entire life looming around the corner, I needed things done quickly and with as little fanfare as possible.

On Friday, January 30, I called Kristen from my office to make sure that we were all set to marry on Monday. "Did you get it done?" I asked.

"Yes. The paperwork is filed, and we are all set. We even met the justice of the peace who will be performing the ceremony!" Kristen said, sounding excited.

"Great," I said briskly. "So we agree. We'll tell our parents and family after it's over, correct?" I wanted to be sure I got to Kristen before our wedding plans were broadcast on the eleven o'clock news.

"My," Kristen paused for a few seconds and continued, "mom . . . ,"

"Oh no. You didn't!" I exclaimed.

"And . . . ," Kristen paused some more, "your mom . . ."

"My mom? I haven't *told* my mom!" My voice quivered.

"My mom told your mom. Our brothers are taking off work and bringing their families. My sister and cousins are coming, too. Arrangements have been made for a sit-down luncheon to follow the ceremony. We have to figure out which wedding party Lizzy is going to be in. She feels torn."

"Wedding parties?" I exclaimed.

Kristen continued. "Cathy and Cousin Kelly are obviously going to be in my party. Your sister-in-law, Maura, will be in yours. So I guess in an effort to keep the parties even, Lizzy should be in yours as well. Though I always imagined she would be in mine. And Gigi will be our flower girl. She'll need to miss school that day. I'll call Sally, or should you?"

"*Kristen! How did this happen?*" I screamed.

"I told my mother, that's how; let's not make a big deal of this," she pleaded.

"Don't make a big deal of this?" I repeated. "I just want my name on our babies' birth certificates. I don't want lunch. I don't want presents. And I don't want wedding parties!" But we were both too pregnant to fight it. Our mothers had taken over and we had no choice but to let them do it. The only way for us to gain back control would be for one of us to go into labor before Monday.

And that's exactly what happened.

Chapter 12

Beautiful Child

Kristen

It was ten o'clock at night and we had just returned home from my dad's birthday dinner when my phone rang. "Hi, Kristen, I got your page," the doctor said over the din of voices. It sounded like she was out with friends at a bar—not the most comforting vision under the circumstances.

"I was letting our dog out the back door when it felt like I wet my pants a little," I told her. The incident seemed insignificant, but I wanted to be sure we had nothing to worry about.

"Where are you?" the doctor asked.

"Out on Long Island," I responded, figuring she'd tell us to sit tight and give her a call in the morning.

Instead she said, "You'd better come into the hospital to have us check you out. From what you're describing, I cannot conclude that your water didn't break." I looked at Sarah.

"This might be it," I said.

Her eyes widened. "I'll start the car."

Less than four hours after we had left New York City, we were headed back in to see if I was going into labor. This was not how

I'd expected things to go down. I was two weeks away from my due date; all I wanted to do was go to sleep. Instead, I was double-checking my "just-in-case" to make sure it was properly packed. "Should we bring my bag with us?" I shouted to Sarah, in total denial that I might be gone for a few days.

"That's the whole point of packing one, isn't it?" she said. Sarah seemed irritated that my water might have broken. Obsessed with getting her entire life organized before either baby was born, she'd started her maternity leave two weeks before her due date. Her pre-birth to-do list included getting a manicure, pedicure, and haircut; having Tucker groomed; detailing the car; and viewing the year's Oscar-nominated films before the Academy Awards, which were scheduled to air in three weeks. She'd been planning to spend the rest of the weekend writing her wedding vows and going to see *Slumdog Millionaire*—not driving me pell-mell to the hospital.

We had a dilemma. We were both far too pregnant to safely drive a car, but Lizzy's driving was so bad, we felt negligent letting her behind the wheel with our unborn children on board. So we decided that Sarah would drive us back into the city, nine-months-pregnant belly and all. Once we cut through the tension of Sarah prioritizing her Oscar-movie-viewing plans over our babies' births, the car trip was actually fun. We spent the entire ride making slap-happy jokes about the fact that even though we were allowing Lizzy to "tour manage" our pregnancies, we didn't feel safe having her drive our car. We thought it was hilarious that she'd flown all the way in from L.A. to sit in the backseat of our car and watch an extremely pregnant Sarah drive an extremely pregnant Kristen to the hospital. We also cracked up over the possibility that my water hadn't broken and that we might end up driving into New York City just to have some poor nurse tell me that I'd peed my pants. During the ride, Sarah and Lizzy repeatedly asked if I was okay. I really wanted to report a drastic change in my condition, but I felt totally normal.

"If my water really has broken it's a slow leak, guys," I told them.

This was nothing dramatic, like I had seen on television. I kept apologizing to Sarah and Lizzy for dragging them out at such a late hour on a Saturday night.

"I won't be annoyed in the least if your water hasn't broken," Sarah replied. "Then I'll get to go to the movies tomorrow." I knew her obsession with going to a movie had as much to do with her passion for salty popcorn as it did with seeing a film.

Earlier that morning, she had woken up with a McDonald's craving. It was one we had both managed to avoid for most of our pregnancies. But on this particular morning, we'd indulged ourselves. As we feasted on Egg McMuffins, we discussed the day's agenda.

"What do you feel like doing today?" Sarah had asked. I knew she was setting me up. There was only one right answer to her question, but I was not in the mood to get a manicure and pedicure after breakfast.

"I really want to go to Babies 'R' Us to get mattresses for the cribs," I responded. Sarah was sick of my "baby registry tic," as she called it, but the mattresses were one of the few items yet to be purchased.

"These babies will not need mattresses in their cribs for another three months," Sarah had said. "They're going to sleep together in a bassinet for the first few months, right? But if that's what you want to do with your day, go ahead."

"I can't carry two mattresses back to our apartment," I'd argued. "I'm nine months pregnant!"

"Well, what help will I be? I'm nine months pregnant, too!" Sarah had wailed.

"I am not exposing my unborn child to nail salon fumes," I said, now arguing for the sake of it. "And I am not letting you expose my other unborn child to them either!"

"That's fine with me!" Sarah replied. "If you want to go into labor without a fresh manicure and pedicure, that's your choice!"

We'd reached an all-time low: We were arguing over mattresses and pedicures while eating Egg McMuffins. I should have known, as I reluctantly marched over to the nail salon, that one of us would soon be in labor.

Sarah

Ever since I'd witnessed a terrible car accident a few years back, my confidence behind the wheel had plummeted. I was a nervous driver, but under the circumstances, I had no choice. Kristen was possibly going into labor, and Lizzy drove like a drunkard even when she was sober. As we approached the Queens-Midtown Tunnel I pleaded with Kristen, "Please, do not criticize my driving in the tunnel; I am feeling worried as it is." As we entered the tunnel, I experienced the most intense rush of anxiety I had ever felt. My nine-months-pregnant belly tightened. I felt like an alien was trying to push its way out of my insides. I grabbed my stomach with one hand and kept the other hand on the wheel of the car. Suddenly the term "tunnel vision" made complete sense to me. "*Ahhh!*" I screamed as my body forced my legs to straighten and I partially stood up in the driver's seat.

"What's happening?" Kristen asked, terrified by my outburst.

"The baby just flipped," I cried between gasps of air. "I think the moxibustion worked!" I was elated and thankful the moment had passed.

"You needed to do that as we entered the tunnel?" Kristen said, clutching her heart and starting to laugh. "Are you *serious*? I think I really did just pee my pants."

When we arrived at the hospital, word had reached the maternity ward that the double-pregnant couple was on their way up. As we got off the elevator, the head nurse greeted us. "Which one of you thinks her water broke?" she asked, holding a gown in her hand.

"I do, but she needs to be looked at immediately," Kristen said, pointing to me. "We think the baby she is carrying just moved from transverse position into proper position. Is there any way we can check that?" The nurse handed us both gowns and told us to get changed. We climbed onto two tables right next to each other and started laughing. "If this is your idea of a relaxing double massage, I'll take a pass next time," Kristen said. It was eleven thirty at night and we were exhausted. The nurse examined my belly with her hands, pressing down to feel the position of the baby.

"You can cancel your C-section," she said. "Your baby moved into the proper position." Before I had time to react, she moved on to Kristen, checking under her gown. Holding a cotton swab in her hand, she announced, "If this cotton turns purple, we know that's not pee in your pants." Kristen giggled nervously as she stuck the swab between her legs. "Your water has definitely broken," she said, holding up a wad of purple. "This baby is on its way." Hurrying out of the room to get the doctor, she called over her shoulder, "Neither one of you is leaving here tonight."

Kristen grabbed my hand and said, "Good thing we went for pedicures!"

Kristen

During the tail end of my pregnancy, I was so sick of feeling bloated, emotional, and exhausted, I just wanted it to be over. But as soon as the doctor told me my water had broken, I was overcome with panic. I knew the next time I left that hospital, I would have a baby in my arms and that life as I'd known it would be over—I was heading into the unknown. It was the kind of anxiety you feel when you're strapped into a roller coaster, slowly inching toward the top of a hill, and you can only think, Did I really decide to do this to myself? Get me off this thing!

It was eleven o'clock on a Saturday night; Super Bowl Sunday was the following day. The maternity ward was all but empty—nobody was going into labor that night. Doula Jen told us to call her when the contractions got bad and she would head over. Because the hospital was so quiet, the nurses moved us into a large corner room. Sarah sat in a chair next to my bed, trying to find a comfortable position for herself. Technically, she was due a few days before me, but she took immediate control of the situation and became the "nonpregnant partner," calling our parents to let them know what was happening, plumping the pillows on my bed, and bringing me water.

Over the next few hours, my contractions gradually increased. At first, I felt like I was getting my period. Then the cramps felt a little worse. Then—ooh—they were a little worse than that. But everything was still very manageable. Every so often a nurse would come into the room to monitor the baby's heartbeat. My sister-in-law, Maura—who was married to Sarah's brother—happened to be a pediatric nurse in that very same hospital, and so she frequently stopped by to check on me. The doctor on call that night, Dr. Sullivan, came in periodically to see whether my cervix was dilating. I spent most of the night doing laps around the nurses' station, holding my belly. At three thirty A.M., the cramps started to feel more intense, so Doula Jen came to the hospital. She helped me do stretches and I sat on the birthing ball, rolling back and forth to try to help my pelvis open up. Like a meditation guide, she coached me to breathe.

At six A.M., Dr. Sullivan came into the room and checked my cervix again. "You haven't dilated any further, and now it's getting dangerous since your water is broken," she said. "I'll let you go a few more hours, but after that, I'm going to put you on Pitocin." This was a synthetic form of the naturally occurring hormone oxytocin. It would increase the intensity of my contractions and hopefully speed up my labor process. I was still hoping to have a natural birth, but my baby's health was more important.

"Okay," I said between long exhalations of air.

Two hours later, Dr. Sullivan hooked me up to the drug. Suddenly, I experienced the worst pain I'd ever felt in my life. It was like someone had torn my chest open and proceeded to pull the muscles off my rib cage. Within minutes, I was standing up, gripping Doula Jen in a football hold. We were face-to-face, holding each other's upper arms and making intense eye contact. Every contraction felt like a speeding freight train was bearing down on me; it was impossible to dodge it—the trick was to breathe in such a way that when I got mowed down, I would be able to get back up.

For two hours I endured contractions so extreme I felt like my body was being torn in half. I'm not a screamer, but I gave my lungs an unbelievable workout, yelling for mercy: "Get me out of here! I just want to go home. I miss Tucker!" I was either standing, holding Sarah or Jen, or crouching on the bed, facing the headboard as a nurse tried to coach me through the contractions. I was shaking, trembling, vomiting, and bleeding, and all the while turning to Sarah for comfort. She was my rock; I forgot she was even pregnant. She rubbed my back while Doula Jen rubbed hers; meanwhile, Nurse Amy was yelling, "You've got this; you can do this, Kristen!"

By ten A.M., the freight train was rolling through the station every two minutes. Well beyond the breaking point, I knew I could not take one more contraction. I was long past the point of being able to "visualize a happy space." I imagined I now knew what an Iron Man triathlete must feel like at the end of a race. I yelled, "Get me an epidural—now!"

The anesthesiologist came in and explained the process: "You're going to need to sit perfectly still while I put a needle in your spine, so we'll do this between contractions." He swabbed my back and prepared the needle, when I screamed, "Wait a minute, hold on." Everybody stepped back as another contraction washed over me. Finally, he was able to slide the needle into my spine. "It'll take about ten minutes before you feel anything," he said.

The anesthesiologist was wrong—I felt better *instantly*. I'd gone from a death scene to mild cramps; half the time I didn't even know a contraction was happening. "You've been up for eighteen hours;

you've just run a marathon," Dr. Sullivan said as I relaxed my grip
on the arms of the metal bed frame.

"More like a triathlon," I muttered. "But really, it was nothing."

"Now we need you to get some rest so you can push this baby
out in a few hours." Blessed sleep. She didn't need to tell me twice. I
drifted into a magical slumber as soon as I closed my eyes.

While I rested, my family gathered in the waiting room. Typical
of the Hendersons, everyone was there: my mom and dad, my
sister and her partner, my brother and his wife, my aunt, uncle, and
cousins, as well as Sarah's mother and father. When it comes to my
family, the going wisdom is: There's an event? Let's all go! Once I
woke up, everyone started to visit. Then Dr. Sullivan came in to do
another pelvic exam, which set me off on a fresh round of tears,
since the previous ones had hurt so much. "Please don't stick your
whole hand up my crotch," I said fearfully. What I *really* wanted to
say was, "Get away from me!" But I didn't feel the exam at all. "Word
to the wise," I said in a weak voice as I looked at Sarah, "epidurals
rock."

"You're eight centimeters dilated," the doctor said. "I'm giving
you one more hour, then I'm going to come back and you're going
to start pushing."

One hour, she'd said. In one short hour, I was going to have a son.
The little guy was going to be completely dependent on me. Gone
were the days when I could hop in the van with my band to play a
gig in another state, see a last-minute movie, or even run downstairs
to the corner deli for a cup of coffee. I wanted to bolt from the bed
and go play pool, get Chinese food, or just lie on a bench in the van,
listening to my iPod as we hurtled down some unfamiliar highway.
"Let's play Scrabble!" I said to Sarah. "Didn't we bring the board in
my just-in-case?"

She looked utterly perplexed. "Scrabble?" she said.

"Yes!" I said, now burning with motivation. "Poker, Scrabble,
cards, whatever—anything but sleep. I've got one more hour left

before I become a full-time dairy farmer, breast-feeding around the clock. If I go to sleep now, they're going to wake me in an hour and my life will be over!"

"What about taking a trapeze lesson?" Sarah asked. We started to laugh uncontrollably.

"Or maybe a Bikram yoga class?" I gasped.

"Go to sleep, Kristen," Sarah said as her giggles subsided. "You're going to need it."

Before the hour was up, in came Dr. Sullivan, snapping on her rubber gloves. "Here we go," she said, and pulled me to the bottom of the bed to get me into position. She handed one leg to Amy and the other to Sarah. Doula Jen stood at the top of the bed, rubbing my shoulders and talking me through the birth.

"Do you want a mirror?" a nurse asked.

"Yes," I said, but only so I wouldn't seem like a horrible mother who had no interest in seeing her son come into the world. I never looked at it once.

"Okay, here we go," someone said. "Here comes a contraction: Start pushing!"

"Bear down, we can see his head!" the nurse cried. I screamed myself hoarse as I pushed.

"Here comes another one: five, four, three, two, one . . . *push!*" the doctor yelled. I felt like someone had put a mountain in front of me and told me to move it: There was no way I could. Doula Jen started talking me through the spiritual portion of the program, something I vaguely remembered requesting: "Open mouth, open vagina," she cooed. "Take deep breaths as your son floats through the passage of life."

"I'm on drugs, I've gone the full Western-medicine monty," I heard myself yelling. "Buddha can't save me now!"

The whole time, I was aware of Sarah. She was holding my hand and talking me through it. "You're so close, Kristen," she said, smiling at me.

The nurse said, "Lift your pelvis and bear down and he will be out in a couple of breaths. Now *push!*" I did one more screaming push; I didn't know I had it in me. Suddenly, I felt a rush between my legs, and with it, a feeling of total relief.

"He's here! We got him!" Nurse Amy cried, holding a tiny, wrinkled, wriggling little boy up in the air. From the moment I'd met my baby brother Tommy, I'd dreamed of the day I would have a son of my own. It was only fitting to name him after the uncle who had made me want to have a boy so badly.

"Hi, Thomas, it's so good to meet you," I whispered as the nurse placed him on my chest. He snuggled up against me, then lay perfectly still. Tears streamed down my face. The nurses whisked him away for a moment to clean him and put a little cap on his head, then put him right back onto my chest. Sarah and I kissed his head over and over while rubbing his back, trying to keep him warm.

"He's so beautiful!" Sarah said, smiling through tears. We were kissing him, kissing each other; we couldn't believe this moment had finally arrived.

Sarah

Thomas Tupper Ellis-Henderson was born at 3:25 P.M. I was in awe at what I'd seen Kristen do and at the sight of our new son. No amount of reading, watching birthing videos, or firsthand accounts from Doula Jen could have prepared me for a birth experience like that. I staggered out to the waiting room to make the big announcement but dissolved into tears of joy instead.

"He's here! He's healthy and amazing!" I sobbed into the lens of my father-in-law's video camera as the entire room erupted in applause.

As I turned to head back into the delivery room, my father-in-law shouted out, "Since you've got us here already, Sarah . . ."

Before he could finish the thought, I spun around on my heel and responded, "Not after what *I* just witnessed: This baby is *never* coming out." I then smiled for the camera, but I was not kidding. Watching Kristen give birth to Thomas was beautiful and miraculous. Being nine months pregnant myself, it was also the most terrifying thing I had ever seen.

Kristen

From the moment we had simultaneously conceived, I'd known these babies had made a pact with one another. After all Sarah and I had been through, their same-day conceptions ultimately had very little to do with us. These two souls were clearly predestined to enter this life together. Sarah, of course, thought I was insane, especially when I started relaying my nightly "Kate dreams" to her.

"She's not ready to come here yet," I told Sarah from my hospital bed the day after Thomas was born.

"And you know this how?" Sarah asked as she rested our newborn on her pregnant belly.

"She told me in my dream last night. She'll come when she's ready, but she's not ready just yet." I relayed the dream as if it were reality, which it was, for me.

"What else did she tell you?" Sarah giggled. "Did she mention any lottery numbers? And please remember, you *are* on painkillers."

I continued, ignoring her. "She told me they travel through lives together. And yes, I am trying my best to enjoy this low dose of pain medication they've doled out to me."

"Anything else?" Sarah pressed.

"She told me that nobody knows him like she does, that he was meant to come first," I said. Then I busied myself with the breast pump as I prepared to admit to a part of the dream that was not so believable. "And that his name is Michael." I tried to mumble the last part under my breath, aware that Sarah was trying to poke holes in my story. The only reason the name Michael had even entered the dream was because my old friend from college had just given birth to a son and had named him that a few weeks earlier; I'd seen it on Facebook. But that had nothing to do with the overall message Kate was sending us.

"His name is *not* Michael!" Sarah said, making it clear that she was done discussing the dream.

"When they're five years old and she starts calling him Michael outside in the backyard, we will remember this discussion," I promised.

Later that day, I was released from the hospital. I had a clear vision of what it would be like to bring my son home for the first time. I'd pictured my entire family at the hospital with us as we dressed Thomas in his "coming home" outfit, complete with a knitted baby bonnet from Great-Nana Mary. Sarah would wheel me down to the waiting car while I held our perfectly swaddled newborn son. My father would carry the suitcase, while my mother and sister would bring all the flowers and cards I had received over the course of my hospital stay. Once we arrived at the apartment, Sarah's parents would be waiting inside, cooking homemade soup and hanging "Welcome Home, Thomas!" signs. The doorman would hand us all the well-wishes that had arrived by mail. Everyone would take turns holding the new baby while I recuperated in bed.

Instead, I discovered that Sarah had told my family not to come to the hospital when they'd called earlier that morning. "We can handle it ourselves," she'd told them one by one, though she had no plan for getting her recovering partner and newborn son loaded into a car with all of their belongings while she was nine months pregnant. "I didn't realize you had so much stuff," Sarah said as we were packing up to leave.

"Why would you tell them not to come?" I said. My eyes filled with hormonal tears of despair. I was exhausted. My body ached. I needed to be taken care of, and my enormously pregnant partner was not capable of meeting my needs at the moment.

Lizzy was in our car, circling the hospital's driveway, waiting for us to appear. As we emerged, the hospital security guards began blowing their whistles to rush us along, without offering to lift anything or trying to help our obviously disadvantaged party. Instead, they watched as I tried to cram myself in between our two newly installed baby car seats.

"Why are both seats installed?" I cried out in frustration.

Though there was no good reason to have both car seats installed so early, Sarah had insisted on doing it before either of us had gone into labor. Now she frantically tried to uninstall one seat before I had a complete and utter meltdown on the pavement. But her pregnant belly would not allow her the access she needed to successfully remove the seat, and the hospital security guards were now verbally berating us to get out of the driveway. So I climbed into the back of the car, wrestled my aching body between the two car seats, and rested my injured lower half on top of the cup-holder console for the duration of the bumpy ride home. I sulked the entire way. This was what you would call a worst-case scenario for any woman who had just delivered a baby. I'd counted on my partner to take care of me through my hospital departure. But she needed someone to take care of her. And so the worst three weeks of our dual pregnancy began. Of course, now only one of us was pregnant.

Chapter 13

Anticipation

Sarah

Once Thomas arrived, all eyes were on me. Because Thomas was two weeks early, everyone assumed I was now late, even though I was still two weeks away from my due date. Even *I* believed I was late. Kristen and I set up camp in our studio apartment just blocks away from NYU hospital, so that when I finally did go into labor, the maternity ward would be only a short cab ride away. We would set up a bassinet for baby Thomas in the delivery room. That way, Kristen could feed him every two hours while helping me deliver our baby daughter.

"You girls are absolutely crazy!" our mothers said. They had no issues voicing their opinions. "He's a newborn infant. Hospitals are full of germs!"

"He spent the first two days of his life in the very same hospital," we argued. Knowing our mothers had a valid point, we discussed the issue among ourselves whenever they were not around. "We need to figure this out," Kristen said. "Feeding Thomas every two hours is going to make it really hard for me to help you deliver this baby." Our mothers were right. Unfortunately, our hormonal minds could not come up with a logical alternate solution. Kristen did not want to spend a single minute away from our newborn son and I couldn't blame her. But there was no way I was delivering my baby without her.

We had another problem brewing. Labor had taken a serious toll on Kristen's body. For weeks, she could barely sit up, much less walk. Immediately following the delivery, she'd lost a lot of blood. While we rejoiced over Thomas's arrival, the doctors were in a state of panic, trying to pinpoint the source of Kristen's massive bleed. Kristen had remained relatively oblivious. She knew something was happening to her but was concerned only with Thomas's well-being. The nurse had stabbed her in the thigh with what had looked like a horse tranquilizer, and from the effect it had on Kristen, it worked like one, too. She'd mumbled in a slurred voice, "As long as Thomas is safely here, I don't care if I die." The doctors' initial fear was that Kristen had ruptured her uterus, a potentially life-threatening situation. Later, they concluded she had suffered a severe perineal tear. Kristen believed she would have been better off with the ruptured uterus. Watching her recovery process, I believed it, too.

Doctor's orders were that she remain off her feet as much as possible, and she could not lift anything heavier than five pounds. Considering the fact that Thomas was seven pounds, fifteen ounces at birth, the task proved challenging. Kristen was in need of constant care during her recovery. The only thing I was capable of providing was the looming threat of having to be rushed to the hospital. We were officially in a pickle, and I wasn't allowed to eat it. To avoid lifting Thomas from his bassinet for late-night feedings, Kristen held him on her chest through the night. This also prevented him from crying, allowing me to sleep so I could be well-rested in case I went into labor. Our parents pleaded with us to leave the city and wait for the arrival of baby number two at our Long Island house. I needed Kristen to help me make a decision. The person I'd counted on to help me across the finish line was officially out of commission. She was surviving on painkillers and focusing every spare ounce of energy she had on Thomas. My pregnant partner in crime was gone. I felt completely alone.

The ninth day into our city vigil, I woke up still pregnant—one day shy of my actual due date. Our situation felt dire. I could not let the sun set on one more day without knowing exactly how Thomas would be taken care of when I went into labor. So I started making phone calls. Before noon, I had left messages for five potential baby nurses. By the time Oprah was on our television set at four P.M., Nurse Jen was in our living room. A short, heavyset Jamaican woman, dressed in nursing scrubs with rubber Crocs on her feet, she stood at the entrance of our studio, shaking her head in disbelief. "We can make this work," she said in her heavily accented voice. "I tink."

We did not have the budget for Nurse Jen, but we were a family in crisis. We needed a firm game plan in place, and her addition to our team was essential. Kristen would pump enough breast milk to feed baby Thomas, enabling Nurse Jen to stay home with him, rather than dragging our newborn infant onto the front lines of my labor and delivery. Our parents made no secret of their great relief and we felt the same. We would all remain in the studio apartment, together, until I went into labor. That way, Kristen would be in close proximity to Thomas should Nurse Jen run out of breast milk. There was only one kink in our plan: Nurse Jen snored like a chain saw. One night confined to our studio apartment with her proved one too many. I called an emergency strategy meeting in our bathroom.

"*We have to* make her wear one of those snoring strips!" I hissed. I was not leaving New York City until after my baby arrived. Kristen laughed at me.

"*We have to* go out to the Long Island house now," she said. "When you go into labor, we will drive into the city and drop baby Thomas and Nurse Jen at the apartment." I couldn't argue with the logic of heading back to Long Island. So on my actual due date, Kristen and I packed up our studio apartment, loaded up the car, and relocated to the suburbs.

Kristen

In the mornings, Nurse Jen and I whiled away the hours passing Thomas back and forth. I would feed him, then she would burp and change him. Conversation would often turn to the night's television programming, what we wanted for dinner, or who we thought would be voted off next on the *American Idol* competition. Thomas's huge appetite made Nurse Jen laugh. She was responsible for his overnight feedings, so I would pump milk in preparation. Some nights she'd wake me to come feed him some more.

"You need to come feed this baby," she said, shaking the empty bottle over my head. "He sucked this thing down!"

At two weeks old, Thomas already weighed over ten pounds. Even with Nurse Jen's help, I was overwhelmed with the responsibility of caring for him. My mind would wander off to thoughts of another baby entering this already fragile picture, and I would panic. I was terrified of having to witness a labor so soon after my own, and even more frightened of the responsibility of having another baby under our roof. To think I'd hoped for three or four! I mentally replayed the voices of every critical friend who'd shaken their head at us in disbelief. Now I found myself skeptical, wondering how we were going to do this.

Sarah

I was officially one week late. My mother was calling every hour to see how I was feeling. She was starting to get very worried. "I just want you to have the baby already; this seems like it's dragging on way too long," she would say, agonized.

My decision to hire Nurse Jen had certainly solved Kristen's crisis. She had a new best friend *and* she no longer had to change dirty diapers. With each passing day that I did not go into labor, though, I grew more mentally and physically stressed. We were even paying someone to live in our house to wait with us. Why not add financial stress to my ever-growing list? On Monday, my father-in-law drove me into New York City for my weekly checkup. I could not believe I was attending such an appointment and had no intention of leaving without being induced.

"I will call you from the doctor's office," I told Kristen as I kissed her good-bye. "I am bringing my suitcase with me to this appointment. The next time I cross this threshold, I will have our daughter in my arms!"

Earlier that morning, I'd emerged from our bedroom for the first time after spending the prior forty-eight hours in bed. I was not sick—at least not physically; I was depressed. Leading up to my emotional plunge, I'd bumped into Nurse Jen in the hallway during the night. "You're still here?" she'd said, unable to believe I hadn't gone into labor yet. Those three words triggered a weekend-long sob fest that nothing could stop. Kristen knew she was entering the bedroom at her own risk. I was mad at her for delivering our son two weeks early and for the fact that she could not seem to understand my frustration. "You could have had a C-section three weeks ago," she quipped during one of her brief attempts to seem sympathetic. It was as if she were blaming me for making sure the baby was in the proper birthing position.

"*Get out!*" I said. I threw one pillow at her head and buried my face in another.

At one point, I could overhear Kristen and Nurse Jen having a conversation across the hall. "She's just over-pregnant," Kristen said, as though she knew everything now that she had delivered a baby.

When I arrived at the doctor's office for what I swore would be my last appointment, the staff surrounded me. Everyone spoke at once: "How's Kristen? How's the new baby? We can't believe you're still pregnant!"

"She's fine. He's great. I can't either," I responded in a monotone voice. I wasn't interested in making small talk; I just wanted to get into Dr. Rosenbaum's office so I could convince her to induce my labor. During one of our very first appointments, she'd mentioned that she would induce one of us if the other went into labor; that way, we could deliver on the same day.

"Oh, I would never have said such a thing," Dr. Rosenbaum said insistently when I reminded her of her promise. "All your numbers are normal. Your fluid levels are fine. The baby is perfectly happy and healthy where she is. I'm sorry, but I can't induce you today." I felt my face contort as tears started to rise. As eager as I was to have this baby, I was not comfortable contradicting Dr. Rosenbaum. She was too sophisticated, smart, and intimidating—even though I knew *exactly* what she'd said all those months ago.

I left the office defeated and still pregnant. As soon as I reached the street, I called Kristen. "Didn't she say she'd induce one of us if the other went into labor?" I asked, pressing her. Kristen recalled the comment as more of a quip than a medical course of action to which Dr. Rosenbaum had committed herself.

"I don't think she meant it literally, honey," she said. "I'm sorry." She sounded genuinely sympathetic, and all my cranky feelings disappeared. I couldn't wait to get home to see her and our new baby boy.

The following week passed one second at a time. My mother-in-law delivered Nurse Jen's favorite dinner to our house on a nightly basis: roasted supermarket chicken with sweet potatoes and applesauce. I would end the meal with a piece of chocolate cake, ice cream, and sometimes both. Kristen was no longer interested in dessert. During the weeks we were no longer pregnant together,

I managed to pack on an additional fifteen pounds, while Kristen quickly lost thirty pounds.

When I'd left the doctor's office a week earlier, I could never have imagined I would be returning a full week later for another exam. But there I was, sitting in the waiting room with my sister-in-law Cathy by my side. She had driven me into the city for my appointment so Kristen could watch our son at home. Though she was usually hysterically funny and even more laid-back than Kristen, Cathy was now acting extremely nervous. She was terrified I would go into labor during our trip into the city.

"Please, not on my watch," she begged.

On this particular trip, I did not bother to bring my hospital bag with me. I knew there was no point. My condition had not changed a bit. I felt exactly as I had the week prior: excessively pregnant, with a perfectly content baby nestled inside me.

"Are you sure you don't want to bring your suitcase with you to this visit?" Kristen shouted after me as I left the house.

"I don't need it," I called back to her. "I called the doctor's office this morning. They will not induce me today unless something is wrong. And, unfortunately, nothing is wrong." I was only half-joking, I was so desperate to get this baby out. An hour after I muttered those words, I phoned home. "You're going to need to bring my just-in-case with you," I said. Kristen hung up the phone so fast I could picture it dangling comically from the hook.

Kristen

I ran around the house, grabbing keys, purse, and Sarah's just-in-case. Then I kissed Thomas and said, "Good-bye, little man; I'm going to get your baby sister." In the car ride to the hospital, I replayed in my head the telephone conversation I'd just had with Sarah: "The doctors aren't worried," she'd said. "Cathy and I are going to grab a bite to eat before we head over to the hospital."

"Why would they induce you if they are not worried?" I'd said. "Shouldn't you go straight to the hospital and check in?"

"If I do that, I can't eat anything until the baby is born," Sarah had said, desperate for her last meal as a pregnant woman. "I need to eat something; then I can go push this princess out."

When I arrived on the labor and delivery floor, everyone knew exactly who I was. "Hi, Kristen," one nurse shouted. "She's in the same room you were in!"

As I pushed the door open, memories flooded in. Now that I was not the one in labor, the room looked different: smaller and warmer. Last time I'd been in that room, I'd been half-naked in a hospital gown on my back with my legs in the air. I guess that had thrown my perspective a bit.

"Thank God you're here!" Sarah exclaimed, sounding panicked. "What took you so long?" It was the first time I had driven a car since Thomas was born. Now that I was a new parent, I did take a few extra precautions behind the wheel (let's just say I hovered a few miles an hour below the speed limit). I'd also assumed Sarah was out to dinner with my sister, per our earlier conversation. "I'm just worried," Sarah said. "My fluid levels are low and Dr. Rosenbaum has not been in to see me yet."

"You said on the phone everything was fine. Did you tell me that just so you could go eat dinner?" I asked. I should have known better.

"Yes, I ate," Sarah admitted with a guilty smile. "I don't want to starve to death in here for twenty-four hours like you did! My fluid levels are low. Sorry I didn't mention that earlier. Where is Dr. Rosenbaum?"

As if on cue, Dr. Rosenbaum entered the room. After exchanging a few niceties, she began prepping Sarah for the induction: She made sure she had an IV line in her arm and was hooked up to a machine so she could see the baby's heart rate. As Dr. Rosenbaum explained what she was going to do, she glanced at the monitor. The look on her face alarmed me. "Did you feel that?" Dr. Rosenbaum asked abruptly.

"I felt a little cramping," Sarah admitted.

"That was a contraction," Dr. Rosenbaum said. "We don't have to induce labor—you're already in it."

Sarah

A little more than three weeks after Thomas entered the world, it seemed that Kate was about to make her appearance. By then, I firmly believed I was late for a reason. After watching Kristen go through delivery, my body had gone on lockdown. Now there was no turning back. Doula Jen returned to the hospital and helped me get into a rhythm with my breathing. Now that I'd had a Ms. Homegrown Earthy Crunchy conversion, I wanted to go for as long as I could without having an epidural. It was eleven P.M. when Dr. Rosenbaum once again entered the room.

"I just wanted to see how you were feeling," she said. "How is the pain from a scale of one to ten? Ten being really painful."

"I'm at a five, but I think I have a higher threshold for pain than the average person, so the average person would probably be at a seven," I said.

Dr. Rosenbaum spun around in her seat. With a smirk on her face, she lowered her glasses and shot Kristen a look of disbelief. "Is this the same patient who asked to be hooked up to an epidural for her sonograms?" They both laughed as Dr. Rosenbaum checked the name on my wristband.

"It's amazing what an afternoon with a birth doula can do to a girl," said Kristen. She loved calling attention to my last-minute shift in birth plans.

"I'll break your water, then," Dr. Rosenbaum declared as she rolled her chair toward a sanitized silver tray lined with medical instruments.

I grabbed Kristen's hand, alarmed. "Is that a crochet needle?" I squealed, and rolled into a ball away from the doctor.

"I can't lie to you, average people don't like this procedure," Dr. Rosenbaum explained. I gulped and felt my forehead break out in a light sweat.

"Is it too late to get an epidural?" I whimpered, squeezing Kristen's hand.

"If you have a high tolerance for pain you should be fine," she said as she worked the gothic torture device deep into my cervix.

"Oh my God, that hurts so much!" I yelled as a gush of water poured from between my legs.

"Did you want to revisit that pain-threshold scale?" Kristen asked, laughing.

Almost immediately, my contractions started to kick in. They came on so fast that when one ended there was no time to catch my breath to prep for the next one. Doula Jen was helping me breathe and hum through them, but I was already exhausted and I'd just gotten started.

I went through most of the night laboring on my own without drugs. Meanwhile, Kristen was pumping milk to give to Lizzy, who would run it downstairs to Cathy, who was sitting curbside in a car to deliver it to Nurse Jen out on Long Island. By midnight, my contractions were coming every five minutes, and by four A.M., Dr. Rosenbaum said it was time to administer Pitocin because I wasn't dilating on my own.

"That's fine," I said, "but I *won't* do it without an epidural." The anesthesiologist came to administer the shot, Dr. Rosenbaum gave me the Pitocin, and I spent the next couple of hours in blissful labor—no pain. Dr. Rosenbaum came back at six A.M. for an exam. "You are ready to push, Sarah," she said.

"Oh. Okay. I can do this," I said nervously. After an hour of pushing, I felt so tired I thought I was going to pass out. "I quit," I shouted to Kristen. "I am done. There has *got* to be an easier way to do this!"

"Well, you *were* scheduled for a C-section," she said bravely.

"I hate when you're right," I said through gritted teeth. Then I pushed and groaned and cried. Twelve hours from the moment my labor began, Kate Spencer Ellis-Henderson arrived.

Chapter 14

One Small Year

Kristen

Early on Tuesday morning, I became a mother again, to a precious baby girl. Most of my family received the news via phone call and text message, as they were waking up and heading to work. My in-laws, on the other hand, had been camped out in the waiting room for much of the night. As soon as I rounded the corner to give them the news, I burst into tears. "She's fine, she's here!" I cried. I did not want them to think anything was wrong, but I was so hormonal, exhausted, and emotional that all I could do was sob. When I'd arrived the night before, I'd overheard my sister, Cathy, trying to comfort Sarah in preparation for the delivery.

"The anticipation of it is ten times worse than the actual event itself," she said, speaking with confidence though she'd never gone through labor and delivery herself. She then prodded me to agree with her expert opinion: "Right, Kristen?" I tried to mask the blank look on my face with a smile, but the clenched teeth may have given me away.

As I stood over Sarah's bed, I could still feel the wounds of my own delivery. All I could muster was an unconvincing "Ah, yeah. It's not *so* bad." A few minutes later, I found myself alone with Cathy in the delivery ward kitchen. I smacked her arm. "Labor and delivery is ten times worse than the anticipation of it!"

"Well, you should have lied better!" she said as she smacked my arm back. I had only just turned a corner in my own recovery. A day earlier, I'd finally felt physically and mentally well enough to attend Kate's birth. The fact that Sarah was going into labor the day after my epiphany was just another sign of how these babies were in communication—and in control of our situation the whole time.

Toward the end of Sarah's delivery, I held her hand and screamed, "Keep pushing!" Inside, all I could think was, This is the worst part; I should tell her to stop pushing and *beg* for the emergency C-section. It seemed like only a split second had passed. Suddenly, Dr. Rosenbaum was holding baby Kate.

Sarah was so busy screaming in protest, *"I cannot do this—I'm not pushing again!"* she was unable to hear our newborn baby's cry.

Dr. Rosenbaum laughed and said to me, "Can you quiet her down long enough to let her know the baby is here?"

"Sarah!" I shook her shoulders. "Stop screaming! Kate is here!" Sarah looked at me, dazed. "Katie is here!" I screamed.

Sarah

After I delivered Kate, my body was flooded with hormones; I'd never felt so good in my life. I'd waited so long and had been so scared; then out came this perfect little girl. My parents picked Katie and me up from the hospital and drove us out to Long Island. Kristen had planned a welcome-home party for Kate and me. When I walked through our front door, I could not believe the number of Henderson relatives packed into my living room. Every cousin, great-aunt, and great-uncle along the eastern seaboard was sitting on my sofa eating pizza and cake. Thomas and Kate were oblivious to the day's festivities. The two babies snuggled in their shared

Pack 'n Play bassinet, Kate's arms wrapped around Thomas. He seemed unfazed by her arrival, as if he had been expecting her all along. Before the babies were born, we'd worried about how they would adapt to one another. Right away, it seemed our worries were unnecessary. Kate clung to Thomas like a heat-seeking missile: She wanted to be wherever he was. And he slept through her cries like they were lullabies.

Kate's birth marked the end of Nurse Jen's stay with our family. When Kate and I arrived home, Nurse Jen passed us on the walkway to catch the train back to Queens. It seemed a little unfair that I'd never gotten to experience the benefits of having a baby nurse help me through the late-night feedings. But the expense of a nurse was more stressful than the loss of sleep I had to endure. And I actually relished the late-night hours with my new daughter.

Gigi, now five years old, was ecstatic about the babies. Sally brought her to visit them on the days that they were born. Her reaction to them was priceless: She raced down the hospital hallway, slid into the room on her socks, punched the Purell dispenser, rubbed the gel furiously into her hands, then held out her arms, as if she expected us to drop the babies into them right away.

Kristen and I renamed the two club chairs in our living room our "Edith and Archie chairs"—after the famed living room set in the seventies sitcom *All in the Family*—and, from the moment we arrived home with Kate, became permanent fixtures in them. Our house became a nonstop visiting station, and everyone who came by seemed to have an opinion on how we were handling new motherhood. Whether we asked for it or not, people could not resist doling out their advice, and our parents were no exception.

"You kids survived just fine without people sterilizing themselves before touching you," Kristen's dad said every single time we asked him to use the extra-large container of hand sanitizer we'd placed in the center of the coffee table.

"Are they not giving the babies pacifiers on purpose?" I would overhear my mom ask Kristen's mom. "They need the pacifier to soothe themselves."

"Are the girls *exclusively* breast-feeding?" Kristen's mother asked my mom in a loud whisper. "How are we supposed to feed the babies if they're only getting breast-fed?"

Even my father chimed in. "Why don't they pump so us grand-parents can feed the babies?" he asked Kristen's mom as he peered over the top of his *New York Times* newspaper.

Having raised us successfully, our mothers were also the experts on baby skin sensitivity. "These wipes irritate their skin," they warned us. "Just use warm water and a cloth." Offended that the diaper cream of their generation was no longer the salve of choice, they would exclaim, "Butt Paste? What's wrong with Desitin?"

The criticisms were endless. With the invasion of the "grandsmothers" in full effect, Kristen and I knew we needed to reclaim what little power we had left. So we did what any normal couple would do: We contacted a team of lawyers. Okay, so Rikki and Christina were close friends of ours; they still felt that a legal document of basic laws was the best way to draw boundaries with overbearing grandparents. Anyone breaking the law would be held accountable and forced to leave the premises immediately—or at least to prepare dinner for us. We drew up the list and posted it on the freezer, where the pumped breast milk lived, making it the most visited area of our house:

Sarah and Kristen's Rules to Live By

1. Do Not Drop the Babies
2. Do Not Try to Make a Happy Baby Happier
3. Sleep When the Babies Sleep
4. You Wake It, You Take It

Rule #1 was the Golden Rule. It helped weed out those who were willing to carry the babies up our steep wooden staircase to the nursery. Rule #2 had been written for Kristen's mother, who'd become infamous for entering our house and ripping a baby out of its swing to change a completely dry diaper. Kristen's mother frowned as she stood in front of the refrigerator, reading the list.

"I'll do what I can," she mumbled, "but a baby should not be left in a wet diaper."

Rule #3 was written specifically with the welfare of Kristen and me in mind, but we would need the grandmothers on board to be sure it was applied effectively. Their nap time was our only chance to sleep; it was also our only opportunity to do household chores. The grandmothers were happy to hold and feed babies, but we really needed them to chip in around the house if we were going to make it through our first few months of motherhood.

"Listen, Sarah," my mother stood at the fridge shouting out to me in the living room, "if you need me and Jeanne to vacuum or do laundry while you and Kristen nap, speak up. I don't need to read it on your refrigerator!"

My mother spoke so loudly, Thomas and Kate woke from their nap. Precisely the reason Rule #4 was created.

Kristen

Following the births of the babies, Sarah and I had two issues that needed immediate resolution—issues most families would never have to think about. For starters, we had to adopt our own babies, a process we both found downright insulting. We hired a prominent New York City lawyer who specialized in LGBT issues to handle the process and were told we'd be forced to endure a social worker coming into our home to deem us fit as a family. We told our neighbors Janet and Mike about it over sushi dinner one Friday night, and both were clearly shocked at what we had to do in order to be considered a family. "Send the social worker across the street to our house when they're done over here," Mike joked, trying to lighten the mood. "We haven't changed the fishbowl water in weeks."

And a visit from a county social worker was only one of several humiliations we'd have to undergo. Our lawyer described the adoption process to us in detail: "In order for a same-sex parent to adopt, the biological mother will have to emancipate her baby in the court, and then each of you will be listed on the birth certificates as 'Parent.'"

I pushed myself forward in the chair I was sitting in. "Excuse me, are you saying I will not be listed on Thomas's birth certificate as his mother, but as his parent?" I could almost choke down the bitter pill of not being listed on Kate's birth certificate as her mother, but this new insult felt like too much. "I realize I am expected to just be grateful that I am even allowed to adopt my daughter, Kate, but I have to give up all rights to the son I carried for nine months and gave birth to and no longer be listed as his mother in order for Sarah to adopt him?" The laid-back musician in me had left the building and I spoke to our lawyer with a tone in my voice as if I might erupt.

Having lived through the adoption of her own children, our lawyer responded with great empathy. "The emancipation process is momentary, literally the swipe of a signature from the judge. But during those few seconds, the babies do become wards of the state in order for you both to adopt them. And I do suggest you save the original birth certificates for posterity if you want documentation of being listed as your babies' biological mothers."

Blown away by the barbarity of the situation laid out in front of us, we nonetheless moved forward and petitioned the court to get the process started. We had read and seen stories on TV about gay and lesbian families torn apart by custody battles—where one partner died unexpectedly and their family swooped in and stole a child away from the surviving partner. While we had drawn up wills declaring each of us the guardian of the other's biological child, and we had explicit conversations with our respective families, who were all in total agreement with our wishes for the well-being of our children, we still had a pressing issue. In order for Thomas to be covered by Sarah's health insurance plan, she would have to prove she was taking steps to legally adopt him.

We also were still not legally married, and the longer we waited, the less likely it seemed we'd ever get it accomplished. Exhausted from sleepless nights feeding the twins, we had to prioritize—the adoptions were our most urgent priority. The wedding would wait until our custody issues were resolved and we were both feeling a bit more comfortable in our new roles as mothers.

During those early days, I spent most of my time with Thomas and Sarah spent most of her time with Kate, mainly because we were both breast-feeding. We would switch off from time to time, just to see what it was like and to take advantage of an opportunity to bond with the baby we had not given birth to. But for the most part, we had fallen into feeding-schedule patterns. I think we envisioned those early months to be much more of a joint venture. I wondered how other two-mom families functioned, particularly those in which both mothers had given birth—and if our babies' close proximity in age was the cause of our temporary divide.

Thomas's first few weeks at home were relatively peaceful. He was in a good routine and seemed to be a happy baby. But around his fifth week, he started exhibiting signs of colic. After doing online research, I concluded he was having a reaction to the cow dairy in my breast milk. It would take two full weeks, and a totally altered diet, for me to clear the dairy out of my system completely. During that time, he was gassy and fussing whenever he was awake. The one thing he found comfort in was music—specifically, the singing voices of Barbra Streisand and Barry Gibb. It was not something that could be scientifically explained, but playing that music for him worked with 100 percent certainty. As soon as he heard the 1981 hit song "What Kind of Fool," he would stop crying as if on cue.

And so, Sarah and I set our music player on repeat. The song played nearly six hundred and fifty times before my system was completely dairy-free. Once it was, Thomas was miraculously cured—he no longer fussed or cried. He was once again the happy baby we'd brought home from the hospital. That's why Sarah and I were shocked a few weeks later when Thomas—eleven weeks old at the time—let out a shrieking scream and went limp in my arms. His eyes rolled back, his body was listless, and he looked pale—almost gray. We looked at each other in horror. Without hesitation, Sarah dialed 911. As I stood in our living room rocking Thomas back and forth, the town fire whistle sounded. Within minutes, two fire trucks and three ambulances were clogging our street. Sirens whirred and lights streamed through the windows. Then the episode seemed to pass, and Thomas was suddenly very alert, looking at all the men in uniforms around the room. Clutching him in my arms, I explained what had happened to a captive audience of volunteer firemen, EMTs, and several county police officers. I was strangely calm, partly in denial that anything could be wrong.

"I'm sure I'm overreacting," I said apologetically.

"Which one of you is the mother?" the overweight paramedic inquired, trying to suss out the situation before him. His arms were crossed. I felt judged before I even answered, but there was no time for insecurities.

"We both are," I said, looking him directly in the face. Our town was small, and we had a good chunk of the local fire department standing in our living room. If we thought we'd been flying under the radar in our little hamlet up until that point, we weren't any longer.

"Which one of you is his biological mother?" he said, pressing further, as he and his buddies exchanged sideways glances.

"I am," I declared.

"Only one parent can ride in the truck with him—the other will have to follow us by car," he said as he scooped Thomas up and strapped him into a car seat for the ride to the hospital. In that moment, I became frantic at the thought of being the only parent in the ambulance with Thomas. How could I make any major decisions without Sarah? I stood helplessly in the driveway, turning from the EMT to Sarah, who looked just as distraught as I felt. Suddenly, our neighbors Janet and Mike appeared on our front walkway.

"What can we do? What do you need?" Janet asked. It was such a relief knowing we had neighbors so close by, willing to look out for us.

"Will you drive with Sarah?" I asked. "She's not sure how to get to the hospital."

"Of course," she said, putting an arm around Sarah and leading her to her car. I hopped into the ambulance and took Thomas's little hand.

Every doctor on call that night greeted Thomas as the EMTs wheeled his gurney through the back doors of the emergency room. It felt like an episode of *Grey's Anatomy* in which the intern doctors fight over the exciting cases coming through the doors. Unfortunately, our baby son was the case the doctors were clamoring over. As the interns jogged alongside his bed, the first listened to his heart. He signaled for another to have a second listen. They looked at each other in agreement. I could tell in that moment something was wrong.

"Your son's heart rate is double what it should be," one of them explained. Just as they began to describe a procedure they needed to perform, Sarah rounded the corner. Out of breath but relieved to have found us, she began firing questions at the doctors as if she'd been standing there all along. She'd heard the diagnosis as she was running in.

"How can you tell it's double the rate? You haven't even hooked him up to a heart monitor yet! Who's in charge here? Are you the attending physician? We need her now!"

The intern doctor seemed to ignore her questions. "If you don't mind, we need to speak to the baby's mother right now," he said, turning back to me.

"Wait—she is his mother," I said. "Well, one of them. He has two." It was maddening to realize that even when my child's life was hanging in the balance, I was going to be called upon to explain myself. But explain myself I would—again and again, until the world accepted the fact that we were a family.

The doctor nodded. "Ah, okay. I'm sorry, ma'am." The attending physician entered the room and explained that they would momentarily smother our son with a bag of ice in order to regulate his heartbeat. It was a horrible thing to witness. Sarah and I held Thomas down on the cot while the doctors went to work. His natural reaction was to jump off the table in shock—a "diver's reflex"—which slowed Thomas's heart rate and helped break the abnormal rhythm. After the procedure, Thomas was admitted into the pediatric intensive care unit at Schneider's Children's Hospital on Long Island. Sarah and I took turns keeping vigil next to his crib, where he was hooked up to machines with an IV line running through his tiny arm. He had to stay in the neonatal intensive care unit—or NICU—for five days. Committed to making sure both newborns had one parent with them at all times, Sarah and I rarely saw each other during Thomas's hospital stay. For days, the doctors watched the monitor and read his EKGs until they could be sure they had a correct diagnosis.

Thomas's lead pediatric cardiologist, Dr. Sandell, was a take-charge lady who knew her stuff. No older than Sarah or me, she was a new mother herself, which comforted us. "Try not to look at the other babies," she told us, implying that some of them weren't going to make it. The NICU was a sad and scary place, despite the warmth of the nurses, the professionalism of the doctors, and the fact that we were receiving world-class care.

Thomas was covered in wires from head to toe. His huge eyes looked searchingly around the room, as if to say, "Where am I? How did I get here?" People would come to visit and say things like "Kristen, I'm so sorry," which I hated—that meant something was wrong, and that was something I refused to accept. It would have been so easy to fall apart—looking at my baby in such a vulnerable position tore my heart to shreds—but I went right into survival mode. I had to be his mom.

Over the course of Thomas's hospital stay, Dr. Sandell spent hours with us, going to great lengths to make sure we understood his diagnosis and prognosis. Our baby son was born with a congenital heart defect called supraventricular tachycardia. Throughout the first year of his life, he would need daily medication to control the arrhythmia that had resulted from the condition. We were sent home with a heart monitor and instructed to call a number every day, where experts would read his EKGs. When I was in the hospital, I'd felt surprisingly calm—after all, Thomas was being monitored around the clock by trained professionals. But being alone with him was a different story. I must have checked his monitor every half hour that first week. Thankfully, he didn't have a single episode. It took a long time before I felt comfortable checking him less often; for the first six months, I did it at least once a day. Finally, Dr. Sandell said that he was responding to the beta-blockers and we could do a reading once a week. By the time he turned a year old and hadn't had an episode, Dr. Sandell was satisfied that Thomas had outgrown his condition. We weaned him off his medication and found that he grew more and more alert. The beta-blockers we had him on were not only slowing down his heart rate; they'd been slowing down his whole personality.

During that first year, I learned that nothing else mattered but the health of my family. In hindsight, issues like the band losing record deals and changing members were nothing but tiny blips on the radar. I'd worked all my life to build that band—and I wanted nothing more than for my kids to see that I had a successful career— but Thomas's illness shifted my perspective in ways I couldn't have imagined. After spending time by his side in the hospital, I knew with absolute certainty that I would give my life to save one of my children's. When I was pregnant, people used to tell me that I'd never be the same when my kids arrived. But I had no clue what that meant until Thomas and Kate were here. My heart left my body on the days they were born, and it was now roaming around the earth in them. My only job from now on was to make sure they got through this life okay.

Sarah

During the early weeks of maternity leave, hearing the voice of Pat Sajak coming from my living room and welcoming me to *Wheel of Fortune* meant one thing: It was time to get out the box of Kleenex. No vowels could be bought or sold to stop it—the nightly show ushered in my chronic case of the evening baby blues, which came on like clockwork at seven-thirty P.M. I'd wrongly assumed that depression would strike Kristen in the days following her delivery. After all, she was the artist in the family, prone to moodiness and apt to express her every feeling and emotion. And during the initial weeks of our babies' lives, she *was* expressing her emotions: She was elated, the happiest I had seen her in years. I, on the other hand, was not usually given to depression but found myself falling apart every night. Happiest when I was running a twenty-five-person depart-ment, planning a party for a hundred people, renovating a house, or dealing with pregnancy, I didn't know what to do with myself now that I was living in the suburbs and fully hitting the brakes. I felt too far away from Gigi, so Kristen would text-message Sally behind my back to arrange visits. Seeing Gigi with the babies was one of the only things that would lift the foggy haze that engulfed me. I felt guilty and conflicted about the feelings I was having, especially considering the fact that it had been so difficult to get pregnant in the first place.

The first weeks of motherhood, I felt like one big boob. I was overjoyed to be their mother, but I felt I wasn't accomplishing anything, aside from keeping my child alive. I was used to checking things off my to-do list, finishing projects and starting new ones. Now my life read like the instruction label on a shampoo bottle: Feed. Change. Repeat. And it never stopped! I missed the fast-paced corporate life I had left behind in New York City and the suburbs depressed me. It wasn't difficult to convince Kristen to move back to New York City; she needed a change of scenery, too, and she knew how important it was for me to be closer to Gigi, who was only blocks away from our apartment and would come over regularly to see the twins. So we packed up our family and relocated to our studio apartment in Manhattan. The stay would be temporary, but hopefully it would be enough to shake me out of my funk.

As soon as I smelled the city air, I exhaled with relief. We breezed through the front doors of our Fifth Avenue apartment building, slowing down just enough to introduce the twins to our doorman Freddy. "You look fantastic, Sarah," Freddy shouted as we passed by. "And so do you, Kristen. Congratulations!" They don't have that kind of service in the country, I thought.

As we passed the mailroom, several of the building's maintenance staff shouted and waved: "*Hola*, Miss Sarah! *Hola*, Miss Kristen! Welcome home!" I waved with one hand and pushed the double stroller with the other. Kristen lagged behind, pushing a valet cart loaded with bassinets, swings, floor mats, and other infant essentials. As the elevator arrived to take us up to the sixth floor it was obvious we couldn't fit all of our belongings in one trip. But I would not let the inconvenience deter me. I was back in New York

City and ready to show off my newborn twins to everyone I passed! "I'll meet you upstairs," I said to Kristen as I smiled at a neighbor and wheeled the stroller around so she could get a better look at Kate and Thomas.

After unpacking, Kristen and I headed to our favorite diner for breakfast. Before long, the entire waitstaff had surrounded our table to meet our two new additions to the family. We were causing quite a scene and I loved all the attention the babies were getting. After the initial hoopla died down, a woman approached our table. "I have twins too!" she said, eager to connect. "Mine are much older, of course."

"These twins are brand-new," Kristen replied enthusiastically. We had been practicing at home as to how to handle these public confrontations and Kristen seemed eager to take on her first challenge. She had already veered off script, as our initial response to the twins question was to be, "We consider them twins, but we each carried one." I had faith she'd steer the ship back on course.

"So you're the mother?" the woman asked, pointing to Kristen.

"Yes, I am," Kristen replied. What I considered a half lie was Kristen's half truth.

The woman continued. "They're big for twins! Did you carry full-term? How much did they weigh at birth?"

"They each weighed just over seven pounds and yes, they were full-term," Kristen said, tackling her questions one at a time.

The woman was unable to hide her shock. "Over seven pounds each? God bless you!" She returned to her table, shaking her head in disbelief. I shot Kristen a look. She continued to eat her breakfast, refusing to make eye contact with me. Before I had time to reprimand her, another diner patron approached us. This time I would answer the questions; I planned to teach by example.

"Your twins are absolutely beautiful," the woman said, peeking her head into the stroller to get a good look at our infants. "They are twins, yes? The boy is so much bigger than the girl!"

"That's because they're not exactly twins," I said, throwing Kristen a here's-how-you-do-it look. "We consider them twins, but I carried one baby and she carried the other." The woman's face reddened.

"Oh," she said. "That's . . . a fascinating story." She slunk away from our table as if mortified by my answer.

Kristen smiled at me and said, "Babe, can you pass the salt?" Clearly, we were going to need to read our audiences a bit better.

Just shy of three months into my maternity leave, I returned to my job at *Real Simple*. Coming back to work, I was full of mixed emotions. I wanted to be with my new family all the time but was reassured by the fact that one of Kate and Thomas's moms was at home with them. I was glad I didn't have to leave them at day care or with a stranger. That first day back, my coworkers crowded into my office, peppering me with questions. "Oh my God, you were so late and Kristen was so early, how did it go?" everyone asked. *Real Simple* did a story about my and Kristen's unique pregnancies in the May issue, following us through each trimester up until the births. Now everyone wanted to know the "behind-the-scenes" stories. I showed them photos of the twins and regaled them with stories of the birth, leaving out the graphic parts. It took only one day for my calendar to fill up with back-to-back meetings. By my second day in the office, I was holding meetings with my boss, Grant, while holding a breast pump apparatus under my shirt. "Believe me, I'd prefer not to be doing this *more* than you'd prefer not to be here while I'm doing this," I said as he discreetly glanced at his notes.

Once, I was going over my to-do list with my assistant, the ubiquitous breast pump working away under my shirt, when she yelled, "Don't turn around. The window washers are in the window behind you!" Unable to resist, I snuck a look over my shoulder. Sure enough, a row of men in coveralls were suspended in a lift behind me, drawing their squeegees over the window. Did I imagine it, or did one of them wink at me?

I sighed and turned back to my assistant. "Welcome to my life now," I said.

One surprising side effect of pumping: It's relaxing. Sometimes I would be in a meeting, pumping, when my eyes would start to feel heavy. "Sarah?" I would hear from far away. "About that marketing strategy we were discussing . . ."

"Oh! Yes!" I would say, snapping to attention. Two minutes later, I would feel my chin touch my chest. I was very lucky to be working in an office environment that was supportive of new mothers. In fact, there were so many of us on staff, e-mails would go around on occasion as a reminder: "Please label your breast milk in the refrigerator so the bottles don't get mixed up." Our floor had "privacy rooms" for pumping and a nurse's station on the seventh floor. Even with all those amenities, I dreamed of staying home, simply because I longed to be with my partner and kids. But these were thoughts I didn't even entertain; providing for my family was my job now.

Kristen

I started to feel anxious right before Sarah went back to work. We'd decided I would stay home alone with the babies, but as the date approached, the reality of what I was about to take on started to sink in. "You're going to need help," Sarah had said.

"I want to do it on my own," I'd said insistently. At the very least, I wanted to figure things out by myself first—establish the routine, learn what the babies needed, decide how I liked to do things—*then* we could hire someone. Now I just wanted Sarah to go so I could get started. I'd gotten myself so worked up at the thought of being home alone with the babies, I just wanted it to happen already.

During those first few months, we would drive Sarah to the train in the mornings, then we'd go out for long walks. Spring was in the air and I still had thirty pounds of baby weight to take off. We might spend the afternoon at the mall; some days I'd drive them into the city for an adventure. I became an expert at getting them in and out of the car, strapping the baby bag to my back while juggling their two car seats in and out of their twin Snap-N-Go stroller. I felt there was nothing I couldn't do with the babies in tow. No obstacle was too great.

One day, while visiting friends in New York City, I had an hour to kill before my lunch date. While strolling around Union Square Park, I decided to drop into the Babies "R" Us located across the street. I could always find something I needed there, and on this particular occasion, I was looking for white onesies. While in the elevator on my way up to the second floor, Kate started wailing uncontrollably. It had been about two hours since her last feeding, so when I got off the elevator, I asked an employee where I could feed her. He directed me to the "Mother's Nursery," a room set up in the back of the store with changing tables and sofas. Grateful the room was empty, I lifted Kate from the stroller and readied myself to breast-feed her. Since Sarah returned to work full time, I had fallen into a rhythm in my role as primary feeder of both babies. As I was about to attach Kate for her feeding, it became clear that Thomas was in dire need of a diaper change. As his sister cried to be fed, I plopped her back into the stroller and lifted her soaking-wet and soiled brother from the seat next to her. As I rushed to change not only his diaper but his entire outfit, another customer entered the room to feed her baby. I felt embarrassed; Thomas's diaper was not only messy, it smelled up the entire room. Upon returning him to the stroller, I lifted a very upset Kate from her seat only to realize she, too, needed a diaper change. While I placed Kate on the changing table, Thomas began screaming. He was now two hours from his last feeding, and I was beginning to sweat profusely. As another mother entered the room, she looked at me, my two babies wailing from hunger, having created a stench so offensive it was unbearable to remain in the room. She shook her head and said, "I feel so bad for you."

I was mortified. My son, Thomas, now wearing an off-the-shelf white Carter's onesie with tags still attached, and my daughter, Kate, bellowing from hunger and a diaper rash, did not need anyone's pity—and neither did I! I threw the diaper bag under the stroller, made sure the babies were safely strapped in, and pushed myself backward out the swinging door of the Mother's Nursery room, only to knock my elbow directly into the emergency fire alarm. As the siren blared, a voice came over the loudspeaker instructing everyone to remain calm and move to the front of the store. I raced back to the elevator, hoping not to be noticed or stopped. The doors opened like the gates of heaven. I rolled the stroller in and began frantically pumping the ground-floor button. Once we hit the main floor, I jogged the stroller through the electric doors and headed directly to the Coffee Shop for our lunch date, never once looking back. Maybe Sarah was right, I thought to myself. I needed to find some help.

About a month after Sarah returned to work, the Bangles offered the band a few opening slots: one at B. B. King's in New York City and one at the Calvin Theater in Northampton, Massachusetts. I called my good friend Nini Camps to see if she'd be willing to sit in for the shows. Our bass player, Jen Z., had officially left the group, so I planned to play bass guitar. Nini, a successful singer-songwriter in her own right, could easily slide into my spot as rhythm guitarist. She was incredibly talented and could pick up and play any instrument on earth. The trick would be convincing her to sing lead vocals. It was a job I had no interest in keeping, and if Nini said yes to it, we'd need her to join the band. Nini and I had written a number of songs together in the past few years, so nobody knew the music better than she did. But I knew she was not looking to join a band—in fact, she was talking about getting pregnant herself. "You keep calling me to play these great gigs!" Nini laughed when I told her about the Bangles dates. Just a few months earlier, she'd subbed on bass guitar when we'd played with Joan Jett and the Blackhearts. "You make it hard to say no!"

"So it's a yes?" I said with excitement in my voice. "You'll join the band? You'll sing lead vocals?"

"It's a yes," she said. "But there's something you should definitely know: I'm three months pregnant."

"Pregnancies are the least of this band's worries," I laughed. "Welcome aboard!"

Our shows with the Bangles couldn't have gone better. People unfamiliar with the band had no idea this particular group of us was playing together for the very first time. The shows proved so successful, Nini stayed on as our new lead singer, and she eventually gave birth to a baby son, Marco, in December 2009. Immediately, we landed a new national booking agent, began selling out the rooms we used to play in New York City, and got exciting calls from bands like Sister Hazel, who asked us to appear on their legendary Rock Boat music cruise.

Sarah

I was raised Irish Catholic. I attended Catholic school and went to church every Sunday. While I felt shut out by the Catholic Church's stance on gay issues, I felt strongly that spiritual faith should play a role in my children's lives.

"I'm struggling at the thought of not baptizing the babies," I said to Kristen one morning over coffee. The topic was a real sticking point for me and Kristen. We each had strong and conflicting feelings on the subject—not to mention we felt pressure from both our mothers, who were deeply troubled by the prospect of our babies not being baptized and possibly remaining in limbo.

"The Catholic Church does not accept our family, and I'm certainly not going to lie to them in order to get Thomas and Kate baptized." Kristen began furiously rubbing her forehead as she spoke—a surefire sign we'd broached a topic that was a source of great angst for her. "Isn't your dad Episcopalian? Don't they like gay people?"

Now we'd hit a subject I wanted to avoid at all costs. My father was a strong and devoted Episcopalian; he'd attended a separate church from my mother every Sunday for all fifty years of their marriage. While my parents had no issue with their differing faiths, it was always understood that we kids would be raised Catholic. The possibility of baptizing my children outside of my mother's faith was likely going to be met with more opposition than not baptizing them at all.

One Sunday, while visiting my parents on Staten Island, I capitalized on a rare moment alone with my father. "Dad, turn off the football game for a second," I said. My mother was busy in the living room with the babies, and I knew I'd have only a matter of moments before being interrupted.

"What do you need, Sass?" I could tell by his tone he expected me to ask if I could borrow money.

"I want to baptize the babies at St. John's." My father's eyes lit up with surprise. St. John's was the Episcopal church my dad had been baptized in seventy-five years earlier and where he now acted as a board member and financial adviser.

"Wow! I wasn't expecting that." He lifted his hand to his forehead in confused disbelief. "I don't think your mother will be too happy about this, but I believe this is a decision you and Kristen need to make for your family."

Since Kristen and I had first discussed baptism, we'd attended a few masses at St. Luke's, an Episcopal church in Sea Cliff. While the mass was a bit different from the ones I was used to attending, the core teachings were very much the same—with one major exception. The Episcopal Church did not alienate its gay members. On the contrary, the church opened its doors to us.

My father went on "You should know that we recently hired a new head priest, Father Cole. He happens to be gay and I've told him all about you, Kristen, and the kids." Typical of my father, he'd just decided to mention this to me for the first time. I couldn't believe my ears. Before we could finish our conversation, my mother entered the room.

"What are you two in here whispering about?" My mother looked at me suspiciously. "You need to borrow money?"

While it actually would have been easier in that moment to ask for a loan, my mind was made up with regard to my babies' faith. "Mom, I spoke to Dad about it and Kristen and I would like to baptize the babies at St. John's." There was a long pause. Finally my mother asked, "What does Jeanne think of this?" Kristen's mom, Jeanne, was raised in much the same way my mother was. When we told her our decision to baptize the babies outside the Catholic Church, she was as conflicted as my mother was. So I lied. "She's okay with it."

"Well then I guess I'm okay with it too." My mother sounded resigned—not so much about the fact that her grandchildren would not be baptized Catholic, but because the faith she'd been raised in would not welcome them. "It's just a shame we don't have a choice in the matter."

And so on June 7, 2009, Thomas and Kate, surrounded by their godparents—Aunt Maura, Uncle Tommy, Aunt Cathy, and Uncle Spencer—were baptized at St. John's Episcopal Church. One hundred of their friends and family members celebrated with them afterward at the Richmond County Country Club on Staten Island, and everyone was welcomed.

Kristen

Trying to find time to rehearse while taking care of two babies was harder than I could have imagined. The grandmothers were coming over all the time to help, but neither one could be expected to do it alone, and if one of their schedules didn't line up, I was dead in the water. One day, the band's most recent tour manager, Devon—who was young and cool and covered head to toe in tattoos—stopped by to meet the twins. She played with them for a while, then expressed interest in taking care of them. Having traveled up and down the East Coast with her on several occasions, I was surprised by Devon's love of babies. It's not that I doubted her ability or desire, I just wondered whether she understood what caring for two babies entailed.

At the time, our tour schedule had slowed to a crawl, and I knew she needed the work. "Give her a chance," Sarah said. "She's been such a trustworthy and loyal friend to you and the band." Which was true. She'd sent beautiful gifts for the babies and was always interested in what was going on in my life. Sarah and I ended up hiring her three to four days a week, and she quickly became part of our family. The babies *loved* her—she became their "rock 'n' roll nanny."

In December 2009, Devon arrived at our house preoccupied. Holding her cell phone up, she walked through the front door reading a text message she'd just received. "Tell the women you work for that New York State is about to vote on gay marriage." She read directly from her phone. Devon looked up at me and asked, "Did you know about this?"

Earlier that morning, my Twitter and Facebook accounts were abuzz with the news, but I was busy feeding the babies and unable to really digest the information or make anything of it. Now that Devon was saying it to me in plain English, I almost couldn't believe what I was hearing. I immediately called Sarah at work to tell her the news.

"Kristen, as soon this thing passes, you're taking me and the babies to town hall and making an honest woman out of me!" Sarah knew exactly what she wanted, and I was happy it was still me.

"Afterellen.com is reporting that the hearings are about to take place," Devon shouted from my computer. With the babies down for a nap, we were both eager to watch the outcome of the vote.

Streaming it live on the Internet, we listened to various New York State senators debate my and Sarah's fate.

Unfortunately, of the seven states where gay marriage had been legalized, two (California and Maine) had recently passed referendums restricting marriage to straight couples. And by the time the votes were tallied on the floor of the state senate, it seemed New York overwhelmingly agreed. I called Sarah as soon as the news was final. "We lost thirty-eight to twenty-four. It just feels so unfair."

"One day our kids will see us get married in the state we live in," Sarah said optimistically. "I think we should wait until it's legal here." And so it was decided—our wedding would wait until we could legally marry in New York, and gay marriage would not be up for consideration again until 2011.

As time passed and Sarah and I grew more comfortable in our roles as new mothers, we also became comfortable telling the story of how we got there. It took a few more awkward encounters, but eventually, no line of questioning led to a flagrant lie or one of us leaving out a massive chunk of the truth. And before long, we realized we weren't the only ones with a unique situation.

In my early twenties, I'd worked with a woman named Anne Lane at an ad agency in New York City. Ten years older than me, she'd spoken of her fertility issues freely. I'd attempted to lend her a sympathetic ear, but I was so young then, with little life experience. Had I known then what I knew all these years later, I'm sure I could have been a much better friend to her. Coincidentally, we had both settled down in Sea Cliff, Long Island, with our families. Now, as we walked her golden retriever down my street, she recounted her own journey to motherhood.

Having tried it all, Anne and her husband had decided to adopt a baby girl; they named her Chelsea Elizabeth. When her daughter turned two, they were ready to add a second baby to their family. The adoption agency called with a unique situation. A baby girl was available, but she was not a newborn. She was two years old, just a few months younger than the girl they'd already welcomed into their family. "They're twins, but not exactly twins," Anne explained.

Sarah and I met a gay male couple at a mutual friend's party. They had just become parents of their own set of fraternal twins. They'd hired a surrogate mother as the egg donor; she eventually gave birth to the biological son of one partner and the biological daughter of the other. In essence, they were half siblings, sharing the same genetics on their maternal side, carried in utero together, and born on the same day.

We have yet to run into a couple with the exact same situation as ours, but we have heard stories of lesbian couples conceiving within months of each other. And we continue to meet people who help us shed our old fears about not fitting in.

One day, Sarah and I were sitting at our kitchen table with our neighbors Janet and Mike, debating whether we should join the Sea Cliff Yacht Club. The club sounded much snobbier than it actually was; it had a pool, a dining room, beach access, and a place for those members who owned boats to dock them. "It's just all those membership fees and none of us even own a boat," Janet was saying.

"We'll do it if you do it," Sarah said.

I had been sitting there quietly, listening to the conversation, when I felt compelled to pipe up: "Will they even let a lesbian couple join the yacht club?"

"I already know a lesbian couple who belong," Janet said nonchalantly. "They have two kids." I was stunned. Sea Cliff was tiny and I'd never heard of this couple.

A week later, Sarah and I were standing by our front gate with Janet when I brought up the subject again. "Now that we know a lesbian couple belongs to the yacht club, Sarah and I want to join," I said.

"There's another lesbian couple in Sea Cliff?" Janet asked.

"You said you heard it from your friend! The one whose daughter goes to school with Lily . . ."

She gave a helpless shrug. "Kristen, I'm sorry, I have no recollection of that conversation," she said.

As soon as the idea had become a real possibility it was taken from me. But once the seed was planted, I couldn't let it go. I started telling our other friends in town, "Did you know there's a lesbian couple with kids who belong to the yacht club? When Sarah and I join next summer, we won't be the only ones!" People shook their heads: No one knew who they were. I was starting to believe they were nothing more than an urban myth.

Three days after my conversation with Janet, Sarah and I were down at the beach. We'd pulled into a parking spot so tight you couldn't have fit a stick of gum between the cars. As I was trying to wrestle Thomas from his seat, a woman next to me was simultaneously trying to load her son into her car. We were practically nose-to-nose as we attempted to maneuver around one another. "Excuse me," I said, shimmying past her.

"Oh, sorry," she said as she pressed her back up against her car. "Why don't you take him out of the seat and we'll step around you?"

"Thanks," I said. I turned to my son as he wriggled out of my grasp. "Thomas, come on, big guy, help me out over here."

"Did you say *Thomas?*" the woman said, whipping around. "Oh my God, is this Thomas and Kate?" Sarah now appeared from the other side of the car, holding Kate.

"Yes," Sarah said, perplexed. "Do we know you?"

"No, but we know *you*," she said. "Our friends have been calling us because they thought we'd appeared in a magazine article in *Real Simple*. My name is also Sara and my daughter's name is Kate!" At that point, her partner popped her head up from the other side of the car and waved.

"I'm Allyson," she said. "Nice to meet you."

"You're the couple that belongs to the yacht club!" I cried. If I could have hugged them right then, I would have.

"We don't actually belong, but we have good friends who do,

and we talk about joining every year," Sara explained. There were so many things I wanted to ask, but instead I let the questions whiz around in my head so as not to embarrass "my" Sarah. Will this town be open to my family? Will the teachers at the school be kind to my kids? Are your children happy here? Are we safe in this community?

Instead, I stuck to small talk: "How's the food at the club?" I asked. "Do your kids participate in sailing camp at the beach?"

Apparently, they'd been trying to find us, too; they'd put the Sea Cliff children's librarian, Miss Anne, on the case. "Have they shown up yet?" they kept asking her. So *that* was why Miss Anne had acted as if she'd been expecting us on the day we'd arrived at the library, pulling the kids in a little red wagon. She'd been checking us out, so she could report back to the other lesbian couple. Now the four of us stood in the parking lot, holding our kids and smiling at each other. "Their" Sara and I were ready to head straight to dinner that night; we were trying to keep our emotions under control and not act too excited. "My" Sarah and Allyson were more tempered: You could see they wanted to take a slow approach. The thinking was, just because we're all lesbians doesn't mean we're going to be friends. After chatting for ten minutes, we exchanged phone numbers and e-mail addresses and went our separate ways.

I waited until the following day to e-mail "their" Sara—I had to work hard to contain myself—then I invited them over to our house for a barbecue. The following Sunday, they showed up on our doorstep with their kids, a bottle of wine, and a container of Allyson's homemade guacamole. It felt like we were on a date with another couple, but one that was always being interrupted: None of us could finish a thought because of the kids. The four of us watched our kids play on the lawn. Theirs were a few years older than Thomas and Kate, which gave us a happy picture of what life might be like down the road. A few days later, Sara and Allyson invited us to go out to dinner and see some live music. We all sat around the table, eating Thai food, talking about the schools and how Sara and Allyson felt they were treated as a couple in Sea Cliff.

"Nobody bats an eye; we never have to explain ourselves," Allyson said.

"Well," Sara interjected, "once in a blue moon, when I introduce Allyson as my 'partner,' there might be a really elderly resident who asks if we run a business together." She laughed. "Once I asked the school superintendent to change a form so it would be more inclusive of *all* the diverse families in Sea Cliff—not just the gay ones, but those with single parents or grandparents. They changed it, no questions asked." Allyson and Sara dismantled each of my fears, one by one. I was so grateful to have a family close by that my kids could identify with—and the fact that we got along so well was icing on the cake.

"We're going to see the early showing of *The Kids Are All Right* at the Roslyn Theatre on Friday night—would you like to join us?" Sara said over the phone after our second "date."

Sara met us outside the theater with our tickets, while Allyson saved seats inside. The theater was packed and we were only a few rows away from the screen. As the closing credits rolled, I was overcome by the most surreal feeling. Here I was, living in a small town, only miles away from where I'd grown up, watching a somewhat dramatized version of my life unfolding before me on the silver screen. Sitting next to me was my lesbian partner and our lesbian neighbors.

As we strolled out of the theater on our way to dinner, I turned to Sarah and said, "See, we're totally mainstream. We're not even big news anymore."

Sarah squeezed my hand and said, "I know two little people who think we are."

Kate and Thomas—Christmas Eve 2010

Epilogue

Sarah and Kristen—August 2010

As we watch the twins grow, their bond becomes increasingly evident. They finish each other's gibberish sentences in much the same way their mothers do. They've soothed each other since the first night they spent together in their bassinet. During their first year, Thomas would let Kate drink from his bottle, a prized possession. Kate, in turn, loved to follow him around and pat his bald head. Now, nearly two years old, they spend their mornings giggling together in their cribs, and when not wrestling in fits of laughter they're holding hands for a round of Ring-Around-the-Rosie. They remind us on a daily basis that from the moment they were conceived, this was their story. Not ours.

Acknowledgments

For their love, endless support, and free babysitting we would like to thank: Barbara and Ken Ellis (Deema and Peapa); Jeanne and Frank Henderson (Nana and Pop Pop); Spencer and Maura Ellis; Tom and Klio Henderson; Cathy Henderson and Cynthia Buccaran; Tip and Rosemary Henderson; Georgia Kate and Leelee Groome; Cousins Kelly and Haley Henderson; Matt Henderson and Pete Raio; Miles and Charlie Ellis; Lilliana and Angelika Henderson; Anne and Gene Cuneo; Candi and Ted Auriano; Julie Rader, Nini Camps, Dena Tauriello, Devon DeVitto; Lizzy Brooks; Jude Mallon; and Mike, Janet, and Lily Perrotta.

For outstanding advice, guidance, and inspiration we would like to thank Kristen Van Ogtrop, Arianne Cohen, Larry Weissman, Sascha Alper, Wylie O'Sullivan, Dominick Anfuso, Martha Levin, Leah Miller, Suzanne Donahue, Jill Siegel, Sydney Tanigawa, Beth Maglione, Edith Lewis, Aja Pollock, Laurie Sandell, Paul Pawlowski and Katie Ambrose, Gretchen Koss and Tandem Literary, Grant Schneider, Kevin White, Michelle Lamison, Tamara Stewart, Courtney Brown, Amy Feezor, Erika Mercurio, and Amanda Potters.

Thank you to the team of experts that got us here and continues to keep us moving forward: Dr. Mattingly and the extraordinary team at RMA; Dr. Rosenbaum, Dr. Sullivan, Dr. Gronau, Cindy, and Cityscape OB/GYN; Jennifer Dembo, CCE, CD (DONA); Dr. Basaca and New Health Pediatrics; and Dr. Sandell and the team at Schneider Children's Hospital.

About the Authors

Kristen Henderson is a founding member, guitarist, and songwriter for the all-female rock band Antigone Rising. In 2005, the band was catapulted into the national spotlight when Starbucks and Lava/Atlantic Records partnered to release their debut CD, *From the Ground Up*, in five thousand stores nationwide. She is the mother of two beautiful children and divides her time between strumming guitar on tour with the band and toting two toddlers to Mommy and Me music classes. Kristen lives in Sea Cliff, New York, and never intends to leave.

Sarah Kate Ellis is the vice president of marketing for *Real Simple* magazine and has been a publishing executive for more than a decade, most recently as creative services director at *Vogue*. She is also the mother of two amazing toddlers and divides her time between her high-powered, deadline-driven job and marching around the house singing "We Are the Dinosaurs" with her kids. Sarah enjoys living in Sea Cliff, New York, but insists on relentlessly discussing her hopes of moving back to New York City over sushi dinner on Friday nights with Kristen and their neighbors.